TENNIS

Mark Cox and Charles Applewhaite

Macdonald
Queen Anne Press

A Queen Anne Press BOOK

First published in Great Britain in 1990 by
Queen Anne Press, a division of
Macdonald & Co (Publishers) Ltd
Orbit House
1, New Fetter Lane,
London EC4A 1AR
A member of Maxwell Pergamon Publishing Corporation plc

This book was designed and produced by
Sackville Design Group Ltd
Hales Barn, Stradbroke, Suffolk IP21 5JG

Editor: John O'Hanlon
Designer: Rolando Ugolini
Illustrations: Rolando Ugolini, Luigi Stefanelli
Photography: Tommy Hindley/Professional Sport

British Library Cataloguing in Publication Data
Cox, Mark
    Tennis – (Top Coach)
    1. Lawn Tennis Techniques
    I. Title II. Applewhaite, Charles III. Series
    796. 342'2
    ISBN 0 – 356 – 17886 – 2

Typeset by Hourds Ltd, Stafford, England
Reproduction by Chroma Graphics (Overseas) Pte Ltd, Singapore

Printed and bound in Spain by Graficas Reunidas S.A., Madrid

Contents

Foreword

Mark Cox

The inherent qualities of modern tennis, which can be said to have been invented by Major Walter Wingfield on 24 February 1874, have long ensured its popularity for participants and spectators alike. From its very inception, the appeal of the game has grown steadily, spreading from country to country, until reaching its present status as a pre-eminent international sport.

The evolution of such major events as the Davis Cup, which was inaugurated in 1900, Wimbledon, the United States Open Championships at Forest Hills and the French Open Championships at Roland Garros has served to cement the competitive game and stimulate international appeal.

In our opinion, though, the great catalyst for the development of the sport internationally was the decision by the Lawn Tennis Association in 1968 to open international competition to all. 'Open tennis' removed the distinction between amateur and professional players, allowed prize money to be competed for and created the opportunity for the game to be marketed and promoted aggressively. The timing was somewhat fortunate too, in that the growth of television synchronized perfectly with the great boost the game received when it was opened to the best players. Tennis has proved the ideal sport for television coverage, and its success in that medium was guaranteed.

Few countries now are untouched by the sport, and the top participants have assumed 'megastar' status, becoming heroes in their own countries and consequently generating immense interest in the game at all levels. Just look at the impact of Björn Borg on Swedish tennis, and the impact of Guillermo Vilas in Argentina! And in Germany, Steffi Graf and Boris Becker have already captivated the hearts of their nation by their domination of the international game throughout 1988 and 1989.

Full status for tennis internationally was achieved in 1988 when it was admitted to the Olympics as a full sport. This gave the seal of approval to the game in the many countries of the Eastern Bloc and Third World.

What then are intrinsic qualities of tennis? What gives it such a broad appeal? It is a fine social game – yes. It gives you a physical sense of well being – yes. It is the challenge of trying to beat your opponent, though, which really makes it captivating: 'given my limited resources, how can I outwit, outmanoeuvre and overcome my adversary?' asks the tennis player. It is a game of strategy, tactics, and a cerebral sport; a battle of minds, both your own and your opponent's. These surely are the reasons why the game has such universal appeal.

This book is a little different from other handbooks and training manuals of tennis. It emphasizes the fact that it is the strategy and tactics that excite us, and open our minds, as is to be hoped, to further and better ways of getting the upper hand over our rivals in competition. We must always remember, however, that our ability to utilize the tactics that we want to use are going to be limited by our technical application of them. A small improvement in the way we play our shots – the technique – can open up a wealth of tactical possibilities. Consequently we have included in the book sections on basic strokes, methods of

Charles Applewhaite

practising, aspects of matchplay and mental attitudes to the game; it will be found, though, that the reader is constantly reminded that he or she should relate these to their context in tactical play as embodied in the all important concept of game planning.

The authors would like especially to thank Mr Dudley Georgeson, LTA Professional Coach, for his invaluable advice and assistance in the preparation of this book for publication, and for his co-operation and that of his students in setting up the special demonstration photographs.

So many people come to us and say 'if only I had taken up tennis earlier!' Certainly you do have an advantage if you play tennis from childhood, especially if you aspire to the highest standards, but isn't it better to have come to this great game later in life than not at all? And one of tennis's great strengths is that you can continue to play at any age.

It is the game of a lifetime.

Mark Cox
Charles Applewhaite

Chapter 1 **Why We Play the Game**

The game of tennis has gained in popularity to an extraordinary extent over the last twenty years. Perhaps this has something to do with the fact that it is so ideally suited to coverage by television, with interest in the big tournaments such as the United States Open and French Open Championships, and of course Wimbledon, growing accordingly. However, as well as being such an exciting spectator sport, tennis remains accessible as a participant sport for players of all ages and levels of ability; and with the building of indoor facilities at an unprecedented rate over the past few years, it can be enjoyed all the year round.

This book has been written in the hope of providing players with sound advice and a strong platform for their improvement copecially in the area of matchplay, strategy and tactics. In order to play tennis successfully it is necessary for the player to have a basic understanding of certain vital principles which are often overlooked, especially if perfecting stroke play is concentrated upon solely to the exclusion of all else.

These principles can be summarized as an understanding of strategy and tactics, sound technical ability related to the player's goals and level of development, general physical fitness and stamina and, last but not least, some mastery of the important psychological skills so vital in tennis, from the simplest recreational game to a 'grand slam' final!

In the past instructional books have tended to cover techniques in a systematic way, and only then move on to consider tactical objectives in a general way. There is no doubt, however, that most players can improve their game dramatically by understanding and using the principles of strategy even if they are not able to improve their specific stroke play. Stroke play must be worked on, but it will improve more rapidly in the context of clearly thought-out strategical planning.

The chapters which follow will provide the keen player with a better grasp of tactical reasoning that will enable him to win more matches. Are you one of those players who has a reasonably sound technique but a lesser knowledge of court craft and strategy? If so this book is specifically designed to give you some ideas, suggestions and solutions aimed at overcoming this problem.

Working towards success

The next time you play a match try to evaluate your own performance and see whether there is an area of your game where you are either regularly succeeding, or regularly being ineffective. For example: you are a hard hitter who sends down winners and losers with equal abandon. Could it be that your losers are not the result of faults in your technique, but of selecting the wrong shot at the wrong time? Or perhaps trying a shot that has very little chance of success at that moment in the point?

When you begin to understand the principles behind matchplay you will realise that, at certain times in matchplay situations, the shot you would *like* to play is not necessarily tactically sound and may have very little chance of success. At these moments you should restrain your natural desire to take a chance on a wild gamble, and instead settle for a sensible positive approach which either keeps you in the point; or sets you up for the next shot to be a winner; or sets you up to force the opponent into difficulty.

Experience counts

Why is it so common to see young players who are quite talented in singles, and could probably beat most of the players in their club, but who when it comes to doubles matchplay find difficulty in beating more senior players? The older players are probably less fit and may have a technique no more polished than their juniors. No, the reason is that the young player frequently has not been schooled in the

Opposite: Michael Chang, the 1989 French Open winner, has already shown a mastery of strategy and tactics which belies his years.

tactics and strategy specific to match-play doubles play, with its wide choice of angles, situations and opportunities for percentage play.

Plan for success

In this book you will find a great deal of help in understanding all areas of singles and doubles matchplay. The emphasis is on playing to plan, using knowledge of your opponent's strengths and weaknesses as well as your own, analyzing the prevailing playing conditions, and making these work towards your success.

The 'mental' side of tennis is given prominence. At the top, some players seem to be unaffected by nerves: when they lose a number of games in a row, or even when faced by a series of set-points against them, they seem only to become more determined to win. So much so that when they do win a game, or save a set point, the other player's game visibly falters. Many matches are lost in the player's mind long before his tennis ability has been bettered.

The approach to tennis followed in this book will encourage the reader to play one point at a time, for its maximum enjoyment, for success, and in a spirit of sportsmanship. Having established the basic principles of a sound attitude to the game, with the importance of game plans as a basis for strategy, and the need for a balanced psychological approach, technique is not neglected and the strokes which form the basic mechanics of every tennis game are analyzed, and allied to appropriate practices and drills.

Note

In the text, where the player is referred to as 'he' or 'him' it is of course intended that both women and men should be included. There are differences between the men's and the women's game, but the principles are the same. And in the area of strategy and planning, determination and imaginative play, the authors are glad to admit that women are frequently the superiors of the men!

Opposite: Zina Garrison shows the concentration and determination that have contributed to her success at the highest level in tennis.

Below: Chris Lewis of New Zealand in action against Mel Purcell of the United States on the No. 1 Court during the Wimbledon Championships.

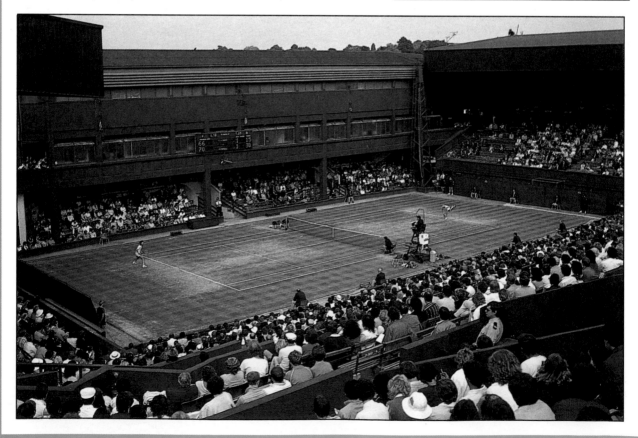

How do we play the game?

Personality

Whenever you watch top class players you will notice how the differences in their personalities seems to reflect the different ways in which they approach the game. When you play tennis you should allow the kind of person you are to decide the way you play. If you are by nature a cautious individual who does not like making mistakes, you will probably be happiest playing steady and consistent tennis. If you like to gamble and enjoy taking risks, you will be more likely to enjoy taking chances on the tennis court by trying difficult shots or going for tricky winners without worrying about the possibility of losing points.

Whatever your character or person-ality, the tennis court is a place for you to be natural, to be yourself. If you can build on the strengths you already possess, you will gain enjoyment from the game and probably have a greater chance of success as well.

Game plans

Game plans are the strategies which players choose to use when playing. A player may decide to play with more aggression than usual, possibly taking the gamble of hitting more winners, but also with the risk of making more mistakes than normally. On the other hand he may choose to be consistent and slightly defensive, perhaps playing with greater care and taking fewer risks. His strategy may swing from periods of attack to periods of mainly defensive play.

Tactics

Tactics are best described as the appli-cation of one's experience and skill in order to gain an advantage over one's opponent or opponents. Fitness, tech-nique and temperament all have an important part to play in the applica-tion of tactics. A tactic is a shot, or series of shots, employed to embarrass an opponent or to make play easier for oneself. It may cover a whole point or be confined to part of the point, so that one point may include more than one tactic, each chosen according to the ebb and flow of the rally.

Technique (stroke play)

Technique is the method of perform-ing the varying strokes used in tennis. As with tactics, the style of stroke play should be the player's own personal choice. The basic principles of tech-nique, which underpin all methods of play, are the foundations which enable players to carry out their tactics effectively.

A sound technique on any particular stroke, one which the player can reproduce time after time, enables him

Below: Steffi Graf, the world's number-one woman player, combines all the necessary components for successful play at the highest level.

to aim the shot accurately into a specific area of the court. To be able to do this is, of course, essential to the success of any tactical plan.

Fitness

All round fitness is a great asset at all levels of play, with its degree sensibly related to age and ambition. Beginners should not be scared off by the thought of strict training; a gentle jog is a good and practical way to start off!

Players need *the four S's*:
● Speed to get to the ball in time to play a stroke in balance.
● Suppleness and agility to jump, bend or turn to gain a good position for a shot.
● Strength for the power shots.
● Stamina so that skill is not reduced by physical or mental fatigue.

All four aspects of fitness are inter-dependent. As stated above, all round fitness, at a level reasonable for the player's personal aspirations, should be the goal.

Temperament

A good and equable temperament is the key to enjoying your tennis. Whenever you play in a singles match, one player must be the winner, the other the loser. By developing a sound temperament you can enjoy the elation of winning without going 'over the top' – conversely, when losing you can meet disappointment without resorting to anger or descending into despondency.

Your temperament will very often be the key to your winning or losing, whether a point, a game, a set or a match. The ebb and flow of a tennis match makes great demands on a player's motivation, determination, flexibility and decision making – by keeping calm and controlled you will be able to make the calculated and rational decisions which are needed if you are to play effectively.

Above: Tennis is a game for all, which gives enjoyment and enhances fitness in addition to being a challenge.

What type of player do you want to be?

Fast court player

Boris Becker is a tremendously exciting player, with his blistering services, ground strokes and net play. He is a great example of success through aggression. He is willing to gamble, so is at his best on a fast surface which brings extra success to the big hitters. His wins at Wimbledon on the fast grass surface which suits him so well and on which he has had consistent success will surely be followed by wins at the same level on slower surfaces like shale or clay once he has learnt to adapt to a more patient game, with protracted rallies. Like all of us, Becker has had to adapt to different playing surfaces.

Slow court player

Mats Wilander, a wonderfully consistent player from the back of the court, is not quite so effective on the faster surfaces. You cannot get into the top ten in the world without being very good on most surfaces. Some clay

Right: Boris Becker, the 1989 Wimbledon men's singles champion, is pictured here playing a very aggressive volley.

court specialists have never been able to change successfully to grass court play, where rallies are shorter and outright winners frequent. Wilander's finest hours have been on surfaces on which he has more time to play his shots with the utmost consistency and accuracy.

All round player

Steffi Graf has succeeded in playing at the highest level on all types of surface. Her game is sound whether she plays on a slow or a fast court. Her naturally aggressive game is tempered with patience when she plays on slower surfaces. She attacks with extra caution, knowing she may become involved in long rallies. On a fast court she can give rein to her natural instincts for the game, enjoying her characteristic power and ability to hit winning shots.

Everything is relative, so whatever your standard you should opt for the type of game which suits your strength and your personal characteristics. If you like a gamble and are aggressive in competition, then model your game on Boris Becker's. If you prefer to invest your money in secure bonds, and are patient, then Mats Wilander may be a more suitable model for you. Consider your physical attributes too; although you do not have to be as big and powerful as Becker to play an effective power game, you do need height and a degree of muscle for this approach. Michael Chang is much smaller, but he can tease his opponents into submission by means of great consistency and accuracy, while tactically probing their weaknesses.

A blend of the extremes is possible. You may prefer an all round game in which ground strokes and net play are equally enjoyed, so evaluate your personal characteristics and plan your game around them. Tennis is an extension of your personality. There is no one way of playing which is better than the others, so develop your game according to the method chosen by *you*, based on *your* individual strengths.

Above: Steffi Graf is an all-round player — she is highly successful on all court surfaces.

Left: Mats Wilander has shown a tremendous consistency of play, especially when playing on clay courts.

Chapter 2 **Tactics for Singles**

There follows a description of the five basic tactics which form the foundation of all players' games, whether they are beginners or world class players. Each of these fundamental areas is described in detail in the following pages, and they should be used to form a sound basis for your match play.

Below: This singles match at Bisham Abbey, the LTA National Training Centre, demonstrates the tactic of making your opponent move on court.

● Master the basic positions in the court.

● Put, and keep, the ball in play.
● Make your opponent move.
● Play on your opponent's weaknesses.
● Wrong-foot your opponent.

Start to practise these basic tactics when you first begin to play and develop them as you improve and play against stronger players. Whichever area of play you work on to improve, stroke play, fitness or temperament,

the result will be a greater ability to employ tactics successfully, and successful tactical play in turn results in winning games.

One of the great joys of competing is to outwit your opponent or to nullify *his* tactics, either by stubborn defence or by counter attack. Enjoyment and interest are heightened by playing every shot with deliberation, as part of a tactic or counter-tactic, so concentration becomes a constructive activity rather than a chore.

The pleasure of playing well, even if your opponent eventually proves to be better on the day, will come more frequently if all the effort you put into improving mentally and physically leads to purposeful tactical play. You can improve your speed, agility, determination and alertness by practising in tactical situations, such as rallying drills, or return-of-service drills.

The basic tactics should be the foundation of your tennis career. As you gain greater pace and control in your shots, and the ability to aim more accurately, you will continue to rely on them but will be able to develop more sophisticated tactics alongside them. Against opponents of a higher standard you will need to put on the pressure by aiming at smaller target areas nearer to the lines, while getting the ball into and away from those areas more quickly through greater pace of shot.

You may be out-hit sometimes. In later years especially you must expect sometimes to be out-run. But there is no reason why you should ever be out-thought!

Below: World-class play at the French Open Championships where the players incorporate all the basic tactics at a high level.

Court positions – singles

Server's position

The server's base should be about one foot away from the centre mark on the baseline. From a central position you can move as easily to one side as the other to cover the return. As a variation of this basic position, you may occasionally want to move out towards the sidelines, perhaps to slice at an angle to the deuce court or to widen the angle available for a wide topspin shot to the side of the advantage court. But as a general rule, and for maximum effectiveness, serve from a position near to the centre of the court.

Receiver's position

The receiver's most advantageous base is about a yard inside the single sideline and on or near to the baseline. From there you have equal chances of covering the service with the forehand or the backhand. Slightly adjust this base to suit your strengths, keeping a little to the left if you favour your forehand, to the right if your backhand is the stronger side. Adjust too to the type of service you expect from your opponent: if he is a big server you should move back a few feet, but against a weak server move just inside the baseline and be ready to move

Right: The basic serving and receiving positions in singles play are shown here at Bisham Abbey.

Opposite top: Martina Navratilova shows poise and balance while under pressure on her volley.

Opposite below: Boris Becker and Ivan Lendl in attacking positions near the net, playing a point eyeball to eyeball!

The singles court positions

Right: The basic positions for the server and the receiver in a singles match. When serving and volleying, the server should follow the line of ball flight as he moves to the net.

Receiver

Server

forward again to punish any short serves.

The receiver should return to the middle of the baseline after returning the serve. If you are moving to the net area you should keep a little to the left of the line of flight of a deuce court return and a little to its right if your return is from the advantage court. This will give you the best chance of cutting off the server's response to your return.

Serve-and-volley

In singles the server should follow the line of flight of his service ball as he moves up towards the net. You will have to play a volley in mid-court and move in quickly to establish a strong net position, about three yards from the net, astride the centre service line. This position will vary slightly according to the angle of attack, but will give the best coverage for returns from either side.

If you stay back, you should recover balance quickly after serving and move to gain an alert readiness position on, or just behind, the centre of the baseline.

Keep the ball in play

Remember that more points are lost through mistakes than are gained by playing 'winning' shots. The service puts the ball into play, the shots which follow keep it in play, and keeping it in play is a very important game objective. This important basic tactic is not just a negative one, in which the quality of the strokes is sacrificed to caution, with the intention of avoiding mistakes at all costs. Be positive. Play up to, but not beyond, your present skill while concentrating on your accuracy every time you strike the ball.

Let your opponent make all the mistakes

Because most points are lost by errors, give your opponent plenty of opportunities to make mistakes by keeping the ball in play. Do not take needless and therefore unprofitable risks. It is not enough just to get the ball back to your opponent's feet, as even a very erratic performer will not make too many errors if he is under no pressure at all. A fine balance must be kept between recklessness and over-cautiousness – see 'Playing the percentages' on pages 64 and 65.

Develop strokes consistently

Whatever your standard of play, as you develop your strokes you should keep working on consistency. As you improve in pace and aim with your strokes, work on consistency drills at the higher level you have reached. Even world class players do not expect to hit a winner off every ball. They take the opportunities to finish off a point which is going in their favour by the use of controlled aggression, but limiting errors is vital to success, even at the top.

The exciting Arantxa Sanchez, the 1989 French Championship winner, hits spectacular shots interspersed with retrieving shots, with outstanding speed and tenacity. It is her consistency in both attack and defence which forms the basis of her world class game. Among the men, Mats Wilander's consistency has been the main reason for the success he has achieved. On a slower court surface, thanks to the extreme rarity of his unforced errors and his tactical cunning, he has managed to win many matches over opponents who, on past form, would appear to have a stronger and more effective game.

Right: This player is working on ball placement on his serve, which is the key to developing a consistent method.

Opposite: Mats Wilander plays his single-handed backhand from a defensive position.

1

2

Make your opponent move

Aim at the gaps

It goes without saying that your opponent will play better if you place the ball near to him, where he can reach it easily while keeping his balance. Accurate footwork, too, is much easier when only a short distance has to be covered.

Make the other player move by aiming wide of him and into the space available on his side of the court. If he has to dash for the ball he may still be moving quickly and will have to check his stride and recover his balance for the next shot: timing the shot will be made more difficult for him if he has to play the stroke on the run. There is also the possibility that he will either over-run and have to play the shot from a cramped position or, if you have been able to place your shot really wide, be forced to stretch to reach the ball at all.

Obviously you will not get an outright winner every time by aiming wide of your opponent, but the pressure put on his stroke play can lead to unforced errors or weaker returns, which you can then exploit to set up your attack.

Create gaps

Use the tactic of hitting first to one side of the court, then to the other. Each time the other player has to move to reach a ball, a gap is created into which you can aim your next shot.

Below: This singles player, in an attacking position at the net, has been forced into a wide defensive situation.

Similarly, follow a good length ball with a short one, placed into the gap which you have created by forcing your opponent deep into his defensive zone. If he is at the net, aim your passing shot as wide of him as you reasonably can, to draw him to one side of the court. Such a shot may be a winner, but if not you have created a gap on the other side in which to aim your next shot.

Test his stamina

Hitting into gaps will win you points, and it will also cause your opponent to cover far more ground than if you placed the ball within his reach. As time passes he will tire and as tiredness sets in skill, quickness of reaction and concentration nearly always suffer. So at all levels of play, but particularly against a player whom you assess as unfit or slow-moving, *play into the gaps*.

At the highest level of tennis, this tactic of moving the opposing player around the court is played so effectively that both players have to use their very high standards of speed and fitness to cover the court and stay in the point.

Aiming for the gaps

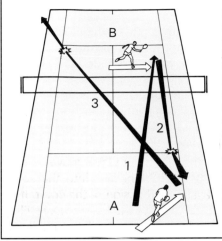

Left: Player A plays a forehand down the line (1) which is volleyed by player B mid-court to a short length (2). Player B is recovering swiftly to cut off the anticipated down-the-line passing shot . However, player A then 'wrong-foots' his opponent by playing the ball back cross-court (3) into the gap for a winner.

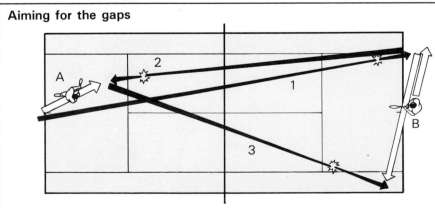

Left: An attacking angle drive has forced this player into a wide defensive situation.

Aiming for the gaps

Left: Player A has hit a deep cross-court forehand (1) forcing player B into his defensive zone. Player B has replied with a short-length return (2) which player A now hits into the gap (3) forcing player B to run diagonally forwards and play his next shot from a wide defensive position.

Play on weaknesses

This tactic is one of the more obvious ones, but it can still be most profitable. If you play more to the weaker groundstrokes or volleys of your opponent than to his stronger side, you will win many points from his mistakes without having to take so many risks yourself. If you have the chance, watch your opponent play before going onto the court with him so that you can assess his strong points and his weaknesses. If you cannot do this, learn as much as you can during the pre-match practice and during the course of the first few games.

Analyze his weaknesses
Try asking yourself these questions:

● Is he stronger at the back of the court than at the net?
● Does he volley well?
● How strong is his smash?
● Is he fast or slow about the court?
● Does he recover quickly after each shot?
● Does he have a weaker side?
● Is he impatient?
● Does he prefer low balls or high?

Exploit his weaknesses
If the opposing player is sound at the back of the court but uncertain at the net, draw him towards the net with short balls and drop shots. Then make him volley, or pass him.

A good volleyer with a poor smash should be pressurized on his smash while you rarely try to play a passing shot to his stronger side. If he is slow, in movement or recovery, stretch him by playing into the gaps, while a few more drop shots than you normally play are likely to win points for you.

Right: Ivan Lendl, in a strong position at the net, puts away a winning smash.

If you are playing against an impatient player, test him by keeping the ball in play, even to the extent of resisting the temptation to try for winning shots early in the rally. Play shots at a medium speed, high over the net and deep to the middle of the court. Capitalize on his impatience, as the longer rallies may well tempt him into attacking impetuously and making errors.

If low balls worry him, use slice in preference to topspin, and the reverse if he is unsure in his handling of balls which bounce high.

Read his game

If one part of his game is not working for him as well as usual, play on this. It may take him some time to realize that he is hitting more losers than winners. Conversely, do not be surprised if he is coping well with a tactic which you expected to work against him. Be ready to alter your tactics according to the situation facing you; after all, if your opponent gets too much practice at one particular stroke he will improve it! Never overplay to a weakness, or your game plan will become predictable and too easy to defend against.

Below: Chris Evert has been forced wide on her backhand and has to play a one-handed rescue shot rather than her normal two-handed method.

Wrong-foot your opponent

This is included among the basic tactics as an introduction to the idea of using *surprise* and *disguise* as weapons. Other tactics can also be made more effective if they are brought in unexpectedly, to catch an opponent by surprise. Disguise too is a powerful weapon as it cuts down the time available for countering your shot. A typical example would be to shape up as though you were about to hit a hard drive, but slow the swing and play a drop shot instead.

For your first attempts at wrong-footing an opponent, try the tactic of hitting first to one side, then to another. Repeat this process, and then instead of keeping to the pattern, hit the ball to the same side twice running. The opponent, expecting the ball to be aimed away from his last position on the court, is likely to have started to move to cover the gap. By playing the ball back to the area he has just left, you can catch him on the wrong foot. He has to pull up, turn and get back again. The resulting strain on his balance and the late recovery can result in him having a difficult shot to play. If you can wrong-foot him thoroughly, he may not even be able to reach the ball.

A similar tactic can be employed against a player who is either at the net or approaching it. You can prepare yourself as though you were going to drive, but play a lob instead. You will have forced him to stop, and to move back to play a smash. He may well have difficulty in getting back under the lob. To play a drop shot instead of the drive will produce a very similar effect where your opponent is at the back of the court.

More sophisticated methods of wrong-footing an opponent include

Below: A successful attack by the net player has resulted in the baseline player being wrong-footed, and leaving a large gap for the winning shot.

playing a deep shot to one side of his court and then a short one to the same side. If he is expecting another long ball he will have to run very hard to reach the short one! Another example is where the ball comes to you high and a smash is expected. Shape up for a powerful smash, but instead play a sliced and softly hit shot down to a sharp angle and into the service area.

As a general rule, do not try to wrong-foot a player who is slow in recovering to the central ready position. You will find that it is more effective to play into the large gaps that he has left open. If you try to wrong-foot the slow player you may find that he is already standing in the best position to return your shot!

Left: This net player has been out-manoeuvred and lobbed successfully.

'Wrong-footing' your opponent

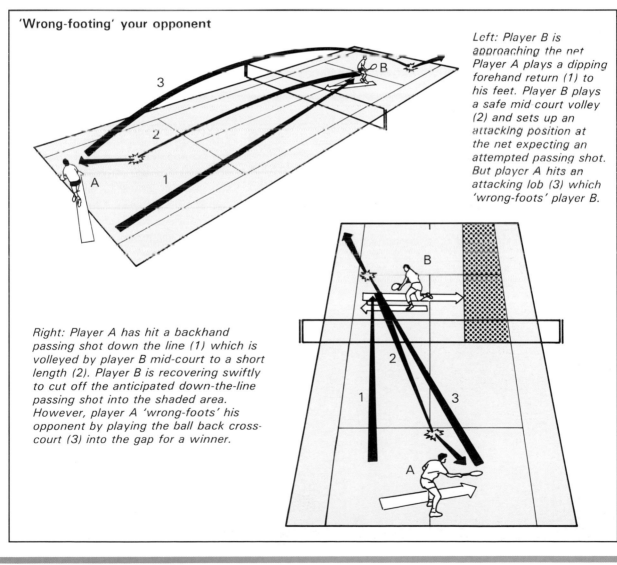

Left: Player B is approaching the net. Player A plays a dipping forehand return (1) to his feet. Player B plays a safe mid-court volley (2) and sets up an attacking position at the net expecting an attempted passing shot. But player A hits an attacking lob (3) which 'wrong-foots' player B.

Right: Player A has hit a backhand passing shot down the line (1) which is volleyed by player B mid-court to a short length (2). Player B is recovering swiftly to cut off the anticipated down-the-line passing shot into the shaded area. However, player A 'wrong-foots' his opponent by playing the ball back cross-court (3) into the gap for a winner.

The zones of court

Defence zone

In general, the area at the back of the court, near to the baseline, is the *defence zone*. From this zone you defend against attack from the net, or rally while waiting to move in against a shorter ball from your opponent.

It is very difficult to hit a winner against an opponent at the back of his court if you are playing from behind or just inside your baseline. Angles are limited when you are a long distance from the net, and even powerful drives have lost their speed by the time the ball has reached the other end of the court. Driving for length and with patience should be the main tactic when you are at the back of the court.

Manoeuvring zone

The middle part of the court is the area from which you can manoeuvre your opponent around his court, as wider angles are available. If your opponent's ball is very short in length, and bounces high, you have a good chance of a sharply angled winner placed close to the sidelines. Alternatively, if the short ball bounces low you can move into the attack with a controlled approach shot, again close to the sideline, and move in towards the net with a good chance to set up a winning volley. The *manoeuvring zone* is an area from which you *may* be able to hit a winner or gain advantage by moving your opponent, but it is not an area in which to stay after you have played your shot. You should generally move forward into the *attacking zone* as quickly as possible to establish a sound base for your next shot. Be wary in case you are lobbed, but be ready to pounce on any return which is suitable for an attacking volley.

Attacking zone

This is the area between the net and the service line. From the net you can volley at a sharp angle, or aim to the side of the court further from your opponent. Or you can play a stop volley if he is well back in his court. He now has less time to reach the ball and set up his next shot, so he is more likely to make an error.

As you move into the attacking zone, stabilize your balance just as the other player hits the ball so that you are ready to move back to cover a lob, sideways for a passing shot, or forward for a volley.

Treat the different zones of the court like a driver at traffic lights. The defence zone is *red*, where you wait for a chance to get going: patience and self discipline are needed here. The manoeuvring zone is *amber* where you get into gear and are ready to let the handbrake off: be ready to proceed with caution. The attacking zone is *green* for go: you are on your way, picking up speed and going for home!

Below: Playing a first volley from below net height in the attacking zone. The player is well balanced and is moving forward to the net position.

The zones of the court

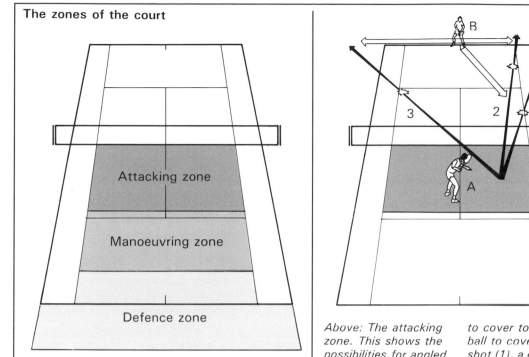

Above: The attacking, manoeuvring and the defence zones.

Above: The attacking zone. This shows the possibilities for angled play for the attacker (A), and the distance that player B might have to cover to reach the ball to cover a drop shot (1), a down-the-line shot (2), and a short cross-court angle (3).

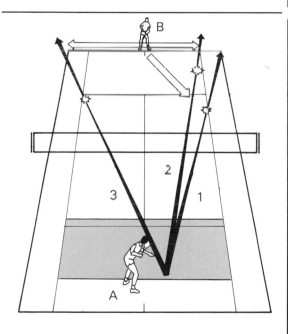

Above: The manoeuvring zone. Here the possibilities for successful angled play by player A are reduced, and player B will have less distance to cover for angle shots (3) and will have more time to reach the ball because of the greater distance A has to hit the ball.

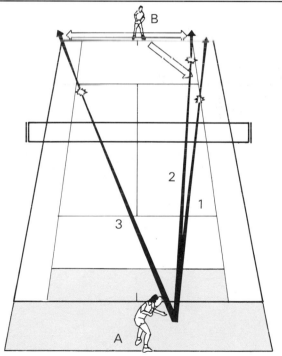

Above: The defence zone. Here the possibilities for angled play for A are further reduced, and the drop shot (1) now has a low percentage chance of success. Player B will have even less distance to cover and more time. Player A should generally hit deep shots to force B into his defence zone.

Chapter 3 **Game Plans**

Below: Martina Navratilova shows concentration and extreme determination.

Opposite: Miloslav Mecir, known as 'the Spider', lures his opponents into difficult situations.

It is through game plans that a player is able to play a sound tactical game, applying the basic principles of strategy to his own particular methods of performance and then further adapting the tactics to overcome the strengths of the opposing player. Game planning is a *must* whatever your standard of play. Build your game plan to gain the most from your own strengths and to bottle up those of your opponent; to cover up your own weaknesses and to exploit his!

The suggestions which follow are chosen as examples from among the many available to you. If you select the tactics which suit the conditions prevailing, you will make the most of your own play while making life difficult for your opponent.

Do not try to include too many individual tactics in your overall game plan: if you do, confusion will arise. But if you get used to thinking tactics, and practise the techniques you will need for them, you will have plenty to choose from when facing different types of opponents in all kinds of different circumstances. Sort out in your mind the benefits you hope to derive from each tactical idea, and which strokes will be required for it. Then design three- or four-part game plans for use against a particular opponent, in particular conditions.

Windy conditions

On a windy day, *give yourself a bigger margin for error*. In the warm up before playing, test out the strength and direction of the wind and play your shots accordingly. This can have the effect of making difficult conditions work *for* you – see pages 68 and 69, 'Using the elements'.

Your opponent's weak strokes

Identify where he is vulnerable, and *play on a weak area of his stroke play.* Try to serve a good proportion of the time to any ground stroke weakness, and when rallying, send the majority of your strokes to this weak side. If the weakness is a serious one, you do not need to employ the tactic of starving it – put him under pressure by playing on it continually. If the weakness is in his volleying, then draw him to the net by feeding him short balls and drop shots, and play on his volley with the most difficult shots you can manage within your own repertoire. If it is his service which gives him problems, threaten it by standing in a little closer than usual and attacking it with determination.

On a slow surface

Be more patient on a slower court surface than on a faster one. On a slower court surface, still play positively and do not give up the urge to attack. However patience will pay dividends. Be prepared to play longer rallies, because your opponent will be able to return shots which on a faster surface might have been winners for you. Risk taking is not so profitable on a slow court, so be more selective in choosing the balls to attack. If your best shots are being returned, do not despair but settle in, and set up for another good attacking position.

Concentrate on first services

Try to *hit a high percentage of your first services into play.* If your first service is unreliable, cut down its pace a little, or aim more into the service court and away from the side and centre lines. If you are getting most of your first services in, this will give you a psychological advantage as well as a practical one. The receiver often breathes a sigh of relief when the server's first delivery goes wide or into the net. His mood changes at once from one of defensiveness to one of aggression, and he looks for a chance to attack. He may move forward a pace or two to show you that he now feels more confident. By getting the first service into play you start in control of the point and have a good chance of maintaining your control right through to game point.

Move the slow opponent

If your opponent is either naturally slow moving, or slowing down because he is tiring, *move him around the court* with the objective of forcing errors from him. A drop shot followed, if he manages to return it, by a lob is a particularly enjoyable tactic. If he then struggles to get to the lob and returns

Below: Stefan Edberg in a perfect ready position, shows the concentration needed prior to returning service. He will already have made plans for attacking any weaknesses in his opponent's service and will be looking for every opportunity to act positively.

it you can then play another drop shot or short ball. Make him run by playing alternately to one side of the court, then the other, adding to the pressure by varying the length of your shots.

Pick tactics to fit *your* plan

In the examples above, suitable tactics are suggested for the particular situations identified, but they are not the only ones which might help to bring about the desired results from the game plan. Much of the enjoyment of becoming an effective tactician is gained from working out your own personal game plans. Consider all the ideas discussed here and you will come to appreciate how top tennis players use strategy and tactics in their game, and learn from watching them in action.

Techniques and tactics

Sound technique is the basis for effective tactical play. All tactics require the ability to play a variety of strokes accurately, so it is necessary to practise these strokes and the movements round the court which link them. For example, if you want to be able to attack at the net after moving in behind a groundstroke approach, you will need the following:
● A deep accurate groundstroke.
● Movement into the volleying area.
● An effective volley or smash as required.

Always practise movements and strokes in relation to a realistic situation, relevant to the tactic you are developing. This will have the effect of improving your technical and tactical competence simultaneously.

Above: Jimmy Connors' high percentage of first serves into play has enabled him to win the major titles on all the fast surfaces.

More game plan tactics

Once you are happy about a number of basic tactics, which can be used in typical situations on the tennis court, and have started to gain confidence with the techniques involved, it is time to think about adding further to your stock of resources. Here are some more examples to choose from.

Vary the pace

To test your opponent's rhythm, *vary the pace of your drives*. He may be successful in dealing with strong, even paced driving; so a slower, higher ball can be a good tactic providing it is hit to a good length. Topspin is better for the higher trajectory drives, while to vary the pace off normal height balls, mix in a slice to take some of the pace off the ball and to provide a different type of bounce for your opponent to handle. You can often cause your opponent to make an error by playing an unexpected spin shot.

Always plan before serving

It is important to *plan your serving tac-*

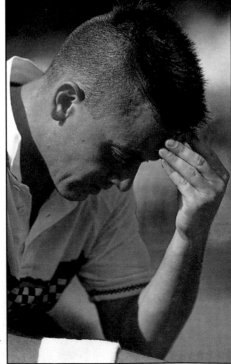

Right: Mikael Pernfors of Sweden is deep in thought at the change-over, probably concentrating on his plan of action for the match.

tics before every service. This tactic will be very successful against a player who is only concerned with his own performance, does not watch his opponent and does not notice any change in his method of play. Ask yourself:

● What type of service shall I use? Choose, according to your ability, from flat, slice or topspin serves.
● Do I want to aim to the forehand or backhand of the receiver, or to his body?
● Do I want to move in to the net or stay back and play from the baseline?

When your mind is settled on these points, and the tactical method clear, you are ready to serve. Repeat this process before *all* serves, whether first or second, until it has become second nature and takes up no more than a moment of time. This moment will however save you from rushing unthinking into an unplanned service.

Do not be rushed

You should never stall unfairly between points or games, but you should *always take sufficient time* to plan and prepare yourself before the next point starts. Some opponents will try to rush you into receiving before you have settled into your ready position. If they succeed you are likely to play a hasty shot without a purpose. If you think this is about to happen simply raise your non-playing arm, the accepted signal for 'not ready', then settle yourself in preparation for your return. Most players will take heed of this signal.

You are allowed up to thirty seconds between points, which is more than enough time to prepare for the next point. If you do not need so long, take only as much as is really necessary.

Use your drop shot

The *drop shot* can be a deadly weapon. Play deep drives: when the

Left: Henri Leconte plays a drop volley using similar racket skills to those he would use for a drop shot.

reply is short, the option for a drop shot is available.

Do not attempt drop shots from outside or near to the baseline. This shot is difficult to judge and play from a longer distance, and by definition the ball will be slow-moving. The further back you play it from, the longer the ball is in the air. Your opponent will have less time to reach the ball, and your shot will have more chance of being a winner, if it is played from nearer to the net.

Play your drop shots away from your opponent, into the gap if he is stranded on one side. This will force him to run on the diagonal instead of straight in to reach the ball, and will take more time.

Always close in behind your drop shot to a couple of yards behind the service line, where you can easily cover a possible return drop shot. If he tries to drive, he will be unable to hit the ball hard because of the nearness of the net, so be very alert as you may need to volley his reply to your drop shot.

Early in the match, it is good strategy to show that you *have* a drop shot. You should not use it very often, but you will have sown a doubt in your opponent's mind as to when it is next going to be played and he will not be able to settle as contentedly on the baseline as he would like. Use it more often if your opponent is tiring.

Use the best percentage shot

On the approach shot, which is the shot you play before moving in to the net to attack, there are three major factors to be considered:

● The angles of play based on the height of the ball, the distance the shot covers and the opponent's position on court.

● Your own ability and confidence in playing the different shots.

● Your opponent's strengths and weaknesses.

These factors should influence your decision making and result in an effective approach shot.

The diagram shows how much you cut down the area you have to cover if your approach shot is down the line as opposed to across the court. The down the line policy should be preferred, but there are times when the cross court approach is a very good alternative. When the opponent has either a weak forehand or a weak backhand, a cross court approach shot to the weak side is likely to produce a poor return which you can then attack at the net.

Bring in the element of surprise. If you regularly approach down the line, your opponent will start covering the shot earlier through anticipation, but if you occasionally hit on the diagonal he will not be able to anticipate so successfully.

When your opponent's shot opens up a very aggressive angled reply from you, go for it hoping for a winner. Follow this shot to the net. It is unlikely to be a strong return under such pressure and you should have the opportunity for an easy volley into an open space.

Opposite: John McEnroe is preparing to serve his now familiar left-handed serve which has been the foundation for his world-class play and success.

Down-the-line and cross-court approach shots

Right: Player A has played a down-the-line approach shot and then moved up to the net. Player B has the two shaded area options available for his passing shots.

Far right: Player A has played a cross-court approach shot prior to establishing himself at the net. Player B now has more time to set up his shot as the ball travels a longer distance than down the line. Because the ball is starting to pull player B wide, he has a larger shaded area down the line into which to aim.

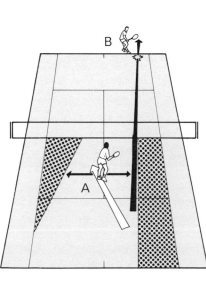
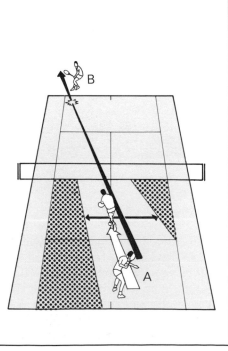

Tactical play

The examples already given show how tennis is not unlike an animated game of chess. The clash between two players' game plans is a mental conflict, just as it is in chess: one player poses a question and the other has to counter with a suitable response. Should he attack or defend? If he chooses to defend, his opponent may be in a position to press home his attack; but defence *is* sometimes the best policy, especially where the chances of making a successful counter attack are slim. In chess, the players have a considerable amount of time to assess the consequences of each move. In tennis the time available for thought during a point is limited to two or three seconds, so quick thinking must be almost instinctive. This ability can only be acquired through practising tactical situations until by repetition the responses have become second nature. It is of little use having a sound technique, in the sense of knowing how to play particular shots well, if you are not able to think rapidly, positively and intelligently, so

make a point of developing this aspect of the game in practice.

Learn from self-appraisement

Tennis practice, including practice matches, should be interrupted and followed by 'inquest' sessions. Decision making is improved by the feedback given during a short discussion with the other players involved, or by a moment taken to reflect on what has happened. 'Was that the best shot to have played, or should I have aimed the ball to a different area?' – 'Was that a missed opportunity? I played a sound, safe shot but a bolder approach might, with hindsight, have given me an advantage; even a winner' – 'I tried for an outright winner but lost the point through an error: was I overestimating my ability to attack that particular ball?' These are the kinds of questions to ask yourself.

Be honest with yourself. Get to know your own tactical strengths and weaknesses. If you have never hit a particular shot well in practice, it is foolish to expect it to work well in a

Right: Rod Laver holds aloft his Wimbledon Singles trophy in 1969. Probably the world's greatest player ever, he has an incredible record of wins on all surfaces.

match. Do not include that particular shot in any tactical plan until you have developed it sufficiently to be able to rely on it in a match situation.

Observe better players

As well as learning through the process of self examination just described, learn from studying more experienced players, whose standard is above your own. You can ask the same kind of questions: 'Why was that tactic successful?' – 'How should he have played to avoid losing that point?' – 'Where will he choose to place his serve at this point in the game?' – 'What sort of shot does he use to approach the net?' This is the attitude of an enquiring mind, which will learn by intelligent observation.

● Remember that good technical strokes only become of real value when there is a purpose behind each one of them. A grooved stroke, plus purpose, equals an effective shot

Below: Chris Evert, seen here in action at Wimbledon, has planned her strategy and tactics to maximize her capabilities during her outstanding career.

Practising parts of game plans

Every game plan includes one or more tactics. As an example, your game plan could be to exploit the comparative weakness of an opponent's backhand. You have decided that his backhand is good enough for it to be unlikely to break down if played on most of the time, so you must put more pressure on it in order to gain profit.

Attack irregularly

Your first tactic is to make your opponent play the backhand while on the run, and irregularly, instead of directing most of your shots to it. If you attack it constantly he would expect your shots to be directed to his backhand and so would have time to prepare well for his shot. Also, the regular practice he would get from consistent attack on his backhand would strengthen the shot. But if you play to his forehand to force him to move wide, and then switch to his backhand, he will have to run further to play his shot. He will often have to play it while moving fast and so less well balanced. Secondly, he will be unaware of when you are going to change from hitting to his forehand to attacking his backhand, as you should be hitting with an irregular pattern.

Keep up the pressure

Under such pressures his comparatively weaker backhand is more likely either to break down, or provide a weak return. To put further pressure on your opponent, exploit the chance offered by a weak return by moving to the net area behind your shot to his backhand, expecting to cut off his shot with a winning volley directed to the other side of the court.

The shots required for these two tactics, and their sequence, should be practised in realistic situations always with the co-operation of a practice partner or a coach.

Practise aiming to one side of the court and then to the other in a regular sequence. Then practise two shots to the forehand followed by one to the backhand of your practice opponent. Thus, with practice, you will be able to vary when you change direction, and so keep your opponent guessing as to when the attack on his weaker side is coming.

Practise following your shot to his

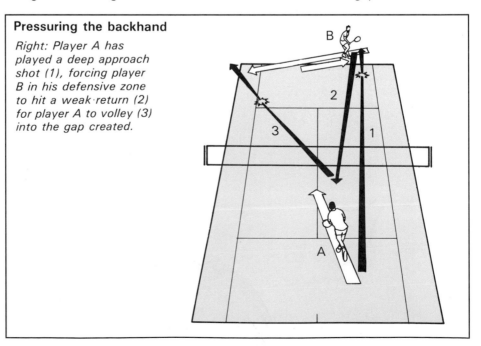

Pressuring the backhand

Right: Player A has played a deep approach shot (1), forcing player B in his defensive zone to hit a weak·return (2) for player A to volley (3) into the gap created.

Left: This player is playing a forceful first volley prior to establishing a strong position at the net.

backhand towards the net The procedure for practising this tactic is examined further at the end of this chapter. If you move in behind the shot to his backhand he may panic into rushing his return, while you are reducing the target area for it. Practise your smash so that when you are being successful at cutting off his returns with your volleys, you are equally well prepared to deal with his probable change of tactic to lobbing.

The shot content of each tactic which you use should be analyzed as above. Only after the practice of shots that are needed for the tactic will the effectiveness of the tactic itself be improved.

Some other tactics to practise

Other tactics may need practice of driving and then lobbing, and the reverse for use once you have driven an opposing net player back with your lob, and need to drive instead of lob-

bing again. Or they may need driving deep to one side and then short and angled to the other side (or the reverse, depending on the situation in the rally); or driving and then drop shotting, remembering to think about when to play the drop shot. Also, you should practise the skill with which you disguise your intentions.

To sum up, with the above as examples:
● Think of a tactic and the shots, and the sequence required for its use.
● Practise the shots separately, and in sequence.
● Think of the returns that could be dangerous from your opponent.
● Practise the shots and positioning in court that will deal with all possible counters to your tactic.

Thus you will gain confidence at playing the various parts of a game plan, and be aware of the possible replies, while armed with the shots that are necessary to deal with them.

Deciding on a game plan

A number of tactics, which can form *parts* of a game plan, have been covered. You should practise these so that you are fully aware of their benefits to you and the possible replies to them which can be expected from an opponent.

In every match you play, a *game plan* should be formulated, based on the strengths and weaknesses of your opponent, the type of court surface and the weather conditions.

Do not change your game drastically

Tennis is a battle of wits between players who are trying to win by hitting the ball over the net and into the court more times than their opponent. If you are by nature a steady, safe player you cannot change overnight into an aggressive serve-and-volleyer.

A wise general elects to fight on terms which suit best the army he commands, and a thinking tennis player keeps as near as possible to the type of game which he enjoys most and which has brought him success in the past. Keep broadly to your favourite kind of play, and adjust it to your game plan so that you get the most from the tactics which you have selected to include within that plan.

An imaginary opponent

You know his game quite well. Perhaps he is a member of your club, or you may have met him a few times in tournaments or matches. He is strong physically, but rather slow-footed. His forehand is a fearsome weapon at club level – very powerful but somewhat erratic.

He does not fancy his chances so much with his backhand, so he settles for a steady slice. When serving, he gambles with a 'one in, six out' first delivery, but the one which does go in is usually a winner. His second service is as sound and unexciting as his backhand, offering little danger but very few double faults. Although quite a steady volleyer he rarely comes to the net, as there he cannot use the one great joy of his tennis playing, his mighty forehand. He has an excellent temperament and is a strong, sporting competitor.

How are you going to beat him this time, after losing closely to him on several previous occasions? The answer may well lie in having a better game plan than the last time you met on the court.

It is a still, fine evening, with the match to be played on your most familiar surface: you will not be upset by the wind or by any change of pace from the court surface. He is a sporting player and will not try to rush you unfairly, so three of the possible choices outlined earlier can be discarded. Before going any further,

Below: Boris Becker, having just won a good point, adopts his now-familiar pose.

select three or four tactics from the remaining ones we have discussed to form a game plan which can be effective against this particular opponent:

- Play on a weakness.
- Get the first serve in.
- Make the slow mover run.
- Vary your pace.
- Plan your serving.
- Use the drop shot.
- Use the percentage approach shot.

The solution

The use of the *drop shot* offers two areas of benefit. It will exploit his lack of speed and bring him to the net, where he is less happy than at the back of the court.

Serve mainly to his weaker side. To ensure getting a high proportion of your serves to his backhand, ask yourself three questions before every service:

- What type of serve?
- Where do I aim?
- Where do I move to next?

Then, balanced and mentally ready, you can take careful aim.

Concentrate on using an *approach shot* down the line, again to his backhand. It should be an advantage to you to play your attacking volleys against a gentle, but not very penetrating, sliced shot.

Move him from one side to the other to take advantage of his lack of speed,

Above: The player in the foreground has just played a forehand approach shot down the line and is moving quickly to take up a strong position at the net.

but do not drive to either side alternately. Make him play two or three backhands and then test him with a wide ball to his forehand, which he may have to play off balance after a long run. Alternatively play one shot wide to his powerful forehand and then angle the next shot to his backhand. This may well force him to play his weaker shot on the move.

Adjust to the standard of play
During the progress of a match, you will be noting how your opponent's strengths and weaknesses are responding. If you are feeling very confident with a stroke or tactic, use it more often and with slightly more aggression than usual. Allow a greater margin of error for shots which are not coming up to their usual standard.

Reverse the procedure in relation to your opponent's game. Starve the shots which he is rarely missing and play relentlessly upon the areas in which he is suffering!

Adjust the game plan during the match
Between points, and particularly at the change of ends, decide which tactics have been working well for you. Continue to concentrate on these without overworking them and becoming predictable. Any tactics which are not proving to be profitable should be used less frequently or discarded. It may be that *your* play on that day is not up to making the most of them, or that *his* play has developed so that he is better able to counter them.

Perhaps your game plan did not have the right elements to be effective against his type of play.

You may see something in his play during the course of the match which could be exploited to your advantage, using a new tactic. *Keep thinking* and be aware of what is happening during the points, and you will be able to adjust your tactical plans quickly and to the maximum benefit.

Opposite: Gabriela Sabatini's formidable topspin forehand provides the platform for her world-class aggressive baseline play.

Below: Henri Leconte, in action at Wimbledon, runs at full stretch to return a wide shot.

Chapter 4 **Advanced Tactics**

Service tactics

When preparing for your service, you have time to consider what tactics you will use. This is the only time in match play when you have a reasonable amount of time to plan your tactics, as during rallies there is never more than a couple of seconds between shots. Use this time well, and try to out think your opponent.

Plan before each serve
● If your level of skill gives you the choice between a flat, slice or topspin service, decide which one you will use.
● Decide whether you are going to serve to the forehand, the body, or the backhand of the receiver.
● Decide whether you are going to serve at maximum pace or at a slower, steadier speed.
● Decide whether you want to serve deep, or short-angle into the service court.
● Plan either to move in behind your service, or to stay back.
● Try to work out your next shot, based on your opponent's expected reply to your service (you should get into the habit of thinking one or two shots *ahead* of your play).

Usually the best policy is to use the flat, and therefore faster, service for your first serve, but vary this sometimes by spinning the ball wide of the receiver. For the second service, mainly use the spin with which you are most confident, changing to an alternative from time to time, to test the rhythm and effectiveness of your opponent's return. Judge the effect on him of your differing types of serve, and if one is proving very effective, use it more frequently.

Play mainly to the weaker side of your opponent. Sometimes a comparison of his forehand and backhand makes it obvious which side you should attack. Exploit that side, but not with every service, or else the opponent will be able to prepare early without having to read the flight of the ball. Keep him guessing. Surprise him with the occasional service to his sronger side.

If the contrast is not so obvious, then you will have to calculate the advantage of serving against a consistent, but not dangerous, shot from one side as opposed to a less consistent, but occasionally winning, shot from the other. Aim your serve to the side which you estimate will be more profitable to you, but if there seems to be very little to choose between the opponent's forehand and backhand returns, then switching from one to the other, frequently but not in a set pattern, is the best policy to follow.

The incoming serve-and-volleyer is more at risk against topspin dipping returns. Move further in to the net against an opponent who can only use slice on one side (usually the backhand), as slice is comparatively easier to volley against. Use the serve-and-volley frequently against opponents who tend to panic and can be forced into wild shots against an incoming server, but beware of using this tactic, except as a variation, against opponents who are cool under pressure and who use dipping shots, or accurate passing shots, consistently.

With practice and experience you will be able to weigh up and decide upon your serving tactics in a matter of seconds. The benefit to be gained from

Left: Ivan Lendl prepares to serve. This is the moment when all his decision-making is crystallized and he prepares to put his opponent under pressure.

Opposite: Before serving, you should decide where and how hard you intend to serve and determine the amount of spin on the ball.

this is clear: when you are serving you will start each point with a considerable tactical advantage if you take the opportunity you are given to *out-think your opponent.*

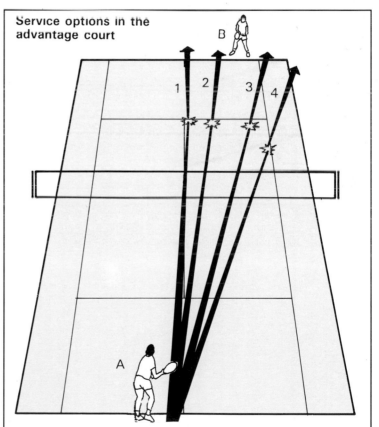

Service options in the advantage court

Above: Service options are as follows:
1 *Down the centre, reducing receiver B's angles.*
2 *Straight at the body, forcing B to move*
away from the ball.
3 *Deep to the corner of the service box, forcing B wide.*
4 *Short angle into the service box, forcing B wide out of court.*

47

Return of service

Below: This player has adjusted his normal receiving position and moved inside the baseline in order to attack a weak second service.

Bottom: The player in the foreground standing just outside the baseline is in a good position to receive his opponent's fast first service.

The time available between the impact of the server's racket on the ball and the moment when your return is made is very short indeed. Boris Becker's opponents have only a fraction of a second to decide upon and make their stroke! But planning *is* possible and if you think intelligently, and above all practise with dedication, the considerations which follow will lead to very quick, almost instinctual, decisions and actions. Keep practising!

• Anticipate the direction in which the server will aim.
• Read the *type* of serve from the server's place-up and body actions.
• Judge the flight of the ball after it has left the server's racket.

Make an outline plan

While settling into an alert readiness position, make your broad plans: for example, 'If it is an easy forehand I will aim down his line; if it is a backhand I will slice low down the middle'. Adjust this rough plan to the actual situation. It might be wiser to play a safer return than you had planned, or you may be able to attack more aggressively than you had expected.

Consider the options

The *type* of shot you play must be based on the *intention* of the return. Take note of whether the server is approaching the net or staying back.

• Drive to attack a weak or short-length serve.
• Drive, but shorten your backswing, against a better service which is nevertheless one that you can attack.
• Semi-attack against a fast, or slightly wide, or heavily kicking service. This should be possible if you have positioned yourself well and have time to do more than play a block return. Slice and good placement may be better objectives than pace and attack in such a situation.
• Block back a service which, through its speed or positioning, puts you under pressure. You may only be able partially to neutralize it, but at least you have made the opponent play the ball again.
• A lob can be used as an alternative to any of these options.
• Use a cross court return as a safe shot, with a good percentage chance of success.

Clearly, your return should be targeted wide of the server whenever this

Left: The player in the foreground is about to return a second service. He is beginning to move to his left in order to gain space to attack with his forehand return.

is practicable. If he is approaching the net, keep your return low, or dipping with spin, so that he is forced to volley upwards. Under pressure it may be wisest to play your return to the safer, larger target area in the middle of the court, always keeping it low. If your opponent is staying back, play a deep cross court return; if you are not under pressure, aim for a weakness.

Work on these points and practise returns of serve stabilizing one point, then another, until you have grooved all of them and are able to react almost automatically when you are receiving. By being able to think and react quickly, and anticipate well, you can turn the position of receiver from one of comparative weakness to one of strength.

Service tactics — options for the return

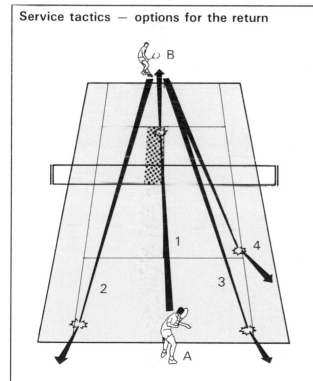

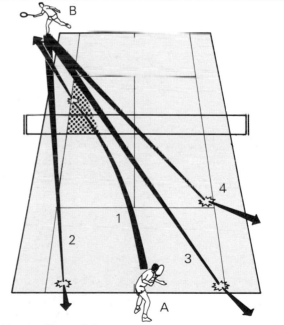

Above: Player A has served down the middle (1) and receiver B has three possible options for returning serve: *deep down the line (2); deep cross-court (3); and short cross-court angle (4).*

Above: Player A has served wide into the shaded area (1) forcing B out of position. This opens up the court for the server's next shot. Player B has three options: deep down the line (2); deep cross- *court (3); and short angle (4). However, if the serve is weak player B will now have time to play an attacking shot (4) and player A will be forced out of position.*

Serve-and-volley

Watching world-class players using the serve-and-volley tactic, is one of the most exciting and dynamic aspects of tennis. Their combination of explosive controlled power on the service, followed by instinctive movement to develop an attacking volleying position is not every player's natural method of play. Many players who have developed their game on slower surfaces use this tactic more sparingly and combine an element of surprise by varying their game and only intermittently following the serve in to the net.

The Americans because of their medium-fast cement courts are generally highly proficient in this area of the game, although at the top of the game all players need to be able not only to serve with speed and accuracy, but to be able to move quickly to dominate the net and intercept the return. Many points are decided in this way, in just three strokes.

Serve-and-volley *(right)*
1 *The server has placed the ball in the air, further forward than for the normal serve.*
2 *Explosive position prior to contact.*
3 *The powerful follow through, already moving into court.*
4 *The acceleration towards the net.*

The strategy

Serve-and-volley is an integral part of the modern tennis game both in singles and, more frequently, in doubles. An accomplished player must be able to use this strategy and know the principles related to it.

In its simplest form, you must put your service into play, run very quickly to the net and play a volley, hopefully for a winner. What are the principles governing this strategy? You should have already decided that you are going to serve and then move in to volley. You are not going to serve, look to see if it is a good serve and then run to the net and volley, because by then you will hardly have managed to get more than six feet into the court before the ball is returned!

It is easier to be successful if the server regularly manages to put the first service into court, perhaps using a little spin for extra control. This is because the opponent generally stands further back to receive the first service. If the server comes to the net on a weak second service, it is the receiver who has the first chance to attack the server.

You should sprint as far as possible up the court to play your first volley. You need to be balanced and comfortable for this stroke, so it is vital that you slow down your run and stabilize your position just as the opponent is about to strike the return. This will enable you to move comfortably and swiftly in either direction to play your first volley.

Attack or defence?

It would be nice to hit a winning shot from the first volley but this is not always possible. How can you tell which volley to attack and which volley to defend? As a general rule, if the volley is low, below waist height, you should try to hit and place the ball deep to enable you to close in to the net and then play your second volley from a strong position for a possible winner. If the return is high and you are playing your volley above waist

height, there is now a chance for you to attack the ball more, either by angling it or playing it with increased power. As a general principle, unless the return is a very easy shot, the first volley should be used to establish a strong position at the net where it should be easier to hit the next volley for a winner.

The objective

The aim of the serve-and-volley tactic is to link together a forceful first service followed by a penetrating first volley, in a smooth and efficient way, to set up a winning situation. The diagram shows one classical way to win by using this attacking tactic: the first volley is not a winner, but the second is.

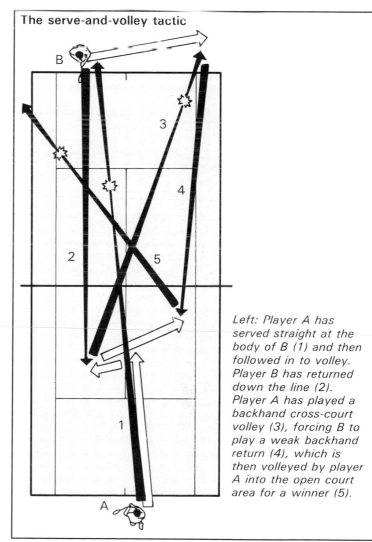

The serve-and-volley tactic

Left: Player A has served straight at the body of B (1) and then followed in to volley. Player B has returned down the line (2). Player A has played a backhand cross-court volley (3), forcing B to play a weak backhand return (4), which is then volleyed by player A into the open court area for a winner (5).

Playing the early ball

Groundstrokes, strokes played after the ball has bounced, are easier to play when the ball is falling from its highest point. The normal method is to move so that you can hit the ball when it is between knee height and waist height. This gives you more time to prepare your swing, while the ball is easier to control, being slow moving and at a comfortable height for hitting. This approach will form the basis for playing groundstrokes throughout your playing career, however far your standard of play progresses. However, there are times when it is profitable to meet the ball nearer to its bounce, while it is still rising, and this is called *taking an early ball*.

The advantages

● You will be playing the shot from a position nearer to your opponent's court, so he will have less time to position himself, and prepare for the next shot.

● It can provide the platform for you to move into the net area. If you want to move up to a strong net position it will be a help if your last stroke was taken from a position as far in to the net as possible.

● The rebound from the faster moving rising ball gives your shot more pace. You can get the same pace with a shorter swing, and this helps ball control and reduces the time taken in preparation.

● Against deep drives from your opponent you will not be forced to move so far back behind the baseline, a position from which you cannot hope to attack. It is a good idea to hold your ground, about a yard behind the baseline, against deep shots, and then move forward to the court to play balls of medium length, rather than waiting behind the baseline for subsequent shots to arrive. You will be playing the early, rising ball, with all the advantages gained from more aggressive tactical play.

The disadvantages

You, as well as your opponent, have

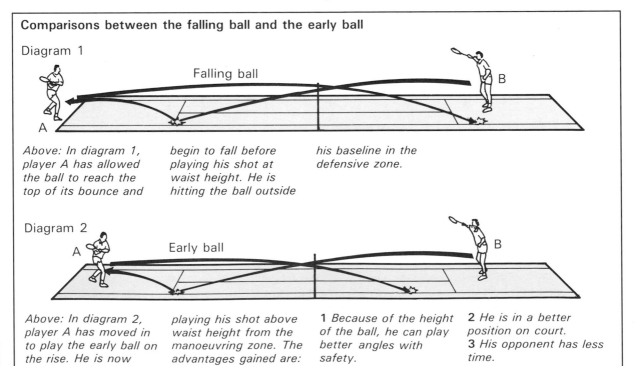

Comparisons between the falling ball and the early ball

Diagram 1

Falling ball

A   B

Above: In diagram 1, player A has allowed the ball to reach the top of its bounce and begin to fall before playing his shot at waist height. He is hitting the ball outside his baseline in the defensive zone.

Diagram 2

A   Early ball   B

Above: In diagram 2, player A has moved in to play the early ball on the rise. He is now playing his shot above waist height from the manoeuvring zone. The advantages gained are: **1** Because of the height of the ball, he can play better angles with safety. **2** He is in a better position on court. **3** His opponent has less time.

less time to prepare for the shot, and an earlier ball is travelling faster and lower than one taken later in its flight. Controlling it is more difficult and challenging. Because you are standing further forward there is a tendency to over-hit and send the ball out of court, so you need to strike the ball more slowly, or with more spin, or lower over the net.

To gain further control, bend your knees and keep your head still at impact. Bending your knees has the effect of increasing the height of the ball in relation to your body and helps you to keep balanced. Keeping your head still also aids balance, and encourages you to watch the ball closely during the shot. Follow through positively, in the direction of your shot, and you will remain well in control of the ball.

Practise taking the early ball, and you will have a tactic in your armoury which brings you into a higher standard of play. Approach each early ball shot with a controlled aggression and it will be found to be an effective method of taking over the initiative and keeping control of the game.

Above: The player in the foreground has taken the initiative by moving into the court and playing the ball on the rise to catch his opponent out of position and set up an attacking play.

Beating the steady player

Some players, without being particularly aggressive or given to playing brilliant shots, are very consistent. They seem to be able to keep on getting the ball back over the net time after time until they win the point because of an error on the part of their opponent. Such a player is sometimes referred to as a 'hacker'! What is the best strategy to use against him?

Adjust your play
Using a game plan requires flexibility in your approach to different kinds of players, but it does *not* require you to alter the style of play which suits you best. Stick with the image you have of your own game, but adjust your game plan's *tactics* to meet the different challenges facing you.

If you are a player who likes to attack where possible, and enjoys taking reasonable risks, and you are drawn against a steady but less powerful-hitting opponent, it would be very unwise to abandon your normal aggressive game and try to out-steady your opponent. You would be providing him with precisely the type of game in which he is most confident, and he would prosper. It would be much better to retain your will to attack, but restrain any impatience, only pressing home your attack after creating a good opportunity to finish the point in your favour.

Be patient
Your game plan against a steady player should be to rally longer than usual, but to attack without inhibition when your opponent has played a weak shot or if you have been able to manoeuvre him from a sound court position.

You should aim to return every service, not by cutting down the pace of your shots but by giving yourself a wider margin of error. The object should be to make him play the ball, not to give him a point by being over-enthusiastic! Remember that although he is not a power player, he can make you work against your own interests if you become impatient or over-ambitious. Do not be drawn into a race with another aggressive player, to hit a winner before the other player does — this can lead to unforced errors.

Keep up the pressure
His advantage is that he is very consistent, yours that you can play more powerful shots. Part of your game plan must be to play on your own terms, using aggression at carefully selected times, when the odds are in favour of success. Miss such opportunities and you will be playing on *his* terms.

Try to get your first service in more often than usual by cutting down the pace very slightly and using a trace of spin for extra control. If you have a useful drop shot, use it to bring him to the net. The steady player is usually less confident at the net, and this tactic will break his rhythm.

Right: Martina Navratilova uses the slice backhand to great effect. She has the ability to develop penetration and to keep her opponent on the defensive with this superb shot.

Get to the net

Against his less powerful hitting you should be able to achieve good net positions from which to exert pressure, placing the ball accurately and playing crisp volleys out of his reach. Be wary, though: this type of player is likely to lob persistently and well, so you may have to play a few steady smashes until a shorter lob gives you the opportunity for a winning smash.

Stick to the plan

Against a player such as this it is important to keep to a winning strategy. If you have managed to place yourself well ahead in the match, using the game plan described above, do not change your plan of campaign. There is a temptation to breathe a sigh of relief – 'I am ahead now, so I shall finish him off!' Put this thought aside, or you may become impatient to hit winners earlier in your exchanges, and may waste vital points by impetuously attacking the wrong kind of ball.

Just as dangerous is the thought that you can maintain your lead, and so win, by playing more safely. 'I *must* hold on to what I have; he is sure to make enough mistakes for me to cruise home.' But is he? The steady player is usually also a determined player: when he is down he is even more determined to return every ball. If you take off the pressure, however slightly, you will give him his chance to climb back into the match.

Keep up the momentum which took you into the lead, by sticking to your game plan, which you have proved effective in practice.

Above: The player at the net has had to move sideways and backwards in order to hit a forehand smash rather than a less strong high backhand volley.

The centre theory

We can all become sound volleyers and effective with the smash, provided we practise well and along the right lines. The next challenge is to be able to move into the net play areas (the attacking zone) either behind a service or a ground stroke approach shot. Broadly speaking, there are three directions for approach shots:

● Roughly parallel and reasonably near to either side line (for ground stroke approaches only).

Right: The player has followed his approach shot to the net and is now playing a well-balanced first volley prior to establishing a net position.

● A cross-court approach shot.
● To the centre of your opponent's court.

The merits of down the line ground stroke approach shots, and cross court approach shots are discussed elsewhere, but cultivate also the centre theory when approaching the net.

Restrict his angles of return

The diagram shows that although the opponent can attempt a pass to either side of the net player he is restricted for space to aim at. The approach down the centre of the court must be deep, as a short length can be punished severely, and the striker has wider angles open to him for a passing shot. Also on a short length approach the volleyer has less time to move to the side to cover and would be hurried in preparation for his shot.

While length is very important for the approach shot, a useful variation is to play a high trajectory shot which will bounce awkwardly enough to make a passing shot difficult for the opponent. In general, play the type of stroke (slice, lift or topspin) with which you feel most confident, and move towards the centre of the net,

The angles in centre theory

Right: The passing areas for a baseline player (B) replying to a short-length approach with the volleyer (A) in a position further back than normal.

Far right: The passing areas for a baseline player (B) replying to a deep centre approach with the volleyer (A) in the optimum central position near the net.

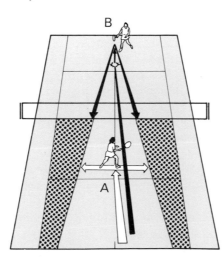

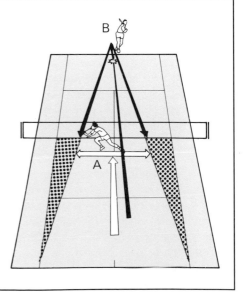

checking for balance just as the opponent is striking the ball. Keep very alert and on your toes, ready to move forwards to volley, or to move back for a smash if you are lobbed.

Your efficiency in the use of the centre theory tactic will be greatly enhanced by practising anticipation, and reading the ball's flight. After such practice, and learning from the experience of using the tactic in matches, you will start to move earlier to cover gaps and to prepare for your shot. This

saving of time is a major factor towards success in net play, when the pressure on both players is intense.

Restrict fast moving opponents

There are players who move very well and so may prefer to play their shots on the run. Make them claustrophobic by using the centre theory against them, restricting their movement. This will reduce the efficiency of their shots and deny them the chance of playing passing shots on the run.

Left: The player at the net, using the centre theory, has played a poor short-length approach shot giving the baseline player an easy opportunity to hit a winning passing shot.

Pressure the net player

If the net player has prepared his approach well, by coming in behind a deep groundstroke or service, he should have gained an advantage over you, his back court opponent.

His position has become the aggressive one, so the baseline player's challenge is to use a counter attack to turn the tables, or at least to level up the situation.

You have a choice of several tactics and must choose the one best suited to the court positions and your confidence in playing the shots needed for the tactic. For example, you may be better at lobbing than playing low, short balls so you should use the lob more than the 'dink' in such situations.

What are the options?

Look for a gap to one side of the net player and hit firmly, but not wildly, at it. Use lifted or topspin drives mostly, although if the gap is wide a firm slice through it can well be the best option. Try to use the method with which you are most confident.

The attempted passing shot may not prove to be a clean pass, but it will take the net player to one side of his court, it may make him play his volley while unbalanced, and it could open up a sufficient gap for a pass to the other side to be a viable option.

The lob is another answer to an opponent who has played a long approach and has moved in to dominate the net. The lob will at least force the net player back; at best, it might win the point outright. If it is played deep enough for the net player to be unable to get back to smash the lob, he will have to chase back to play the ball after it has bounced. Then, having

Below: Ivan Lendl in the attacking position at the net is passed however by a forehand from Boris Becker.

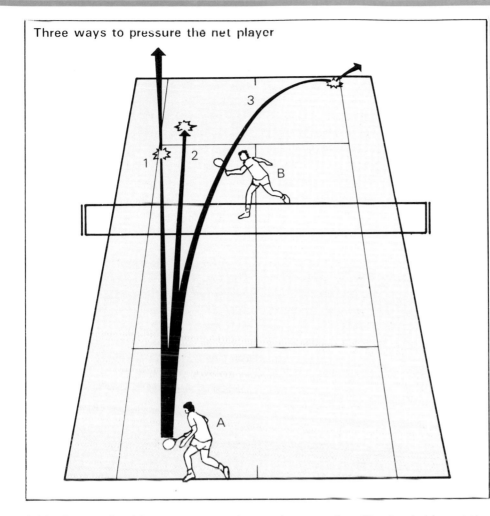

Three ways to pressure the net player

1

2

3

B

A

Left: Three possibilities for pressuring the net player:
1 *A short 'dink', forcing the net player to play a low volley.*
2 *A normal passing shot.*
3 *A lob.*

lobbed, you should move up to take over the net position.

The soft, low drive, or 'dink' to make the net volley is another tactic to use against him. It is a risky one, because if the ball is not played very accurately it may be high enough for the opponent to reply with an easy winning volley from very close to the net. Use slice, or heavy topspin, according to which suits your personal skills better, and move in towards the net to try to pick off the upward volley of your opponent with a counter attacking volley placed wide of him.

Beat the short approach shot

If your opponent's approach shot is short, you should be able to win the point. The passing shot should be much easier, with a sharper angle to the side now available; the lob can be lower and attacking, with heavy top-spin an option. The hard drive at the opponent to give him little time to play a return shot is another good option for you, though against a long approach shot this 'bodyline' attack is of very little value.

Do not panic

Your greatest challenge is a good approach shot from an efficient volleyer. Practise the three main ways to combat him, and vary them as countering tactics, using the one at which you are most confident more often than the others.

Above all, do not panic when faced with a determined incoming volleyer, or one already at the net. Keep calm and play a firm and well chosen shot. By keeping the ball in play you have the chance to regain the initiative on your subsequent shots.

Groundstrokes and net play

The advantages of net play

When two opponents are of about equal ability, the player who uses the whole court, the all-court player, should beat the one who relies almost entirely on playing from the back of his court. There are a number of ways in which the net player can put pressure on his opponent, and the nearer he gets to the net the greater are his opportunities for sharply angled shots to the sidelines.

His shots are played nearer to his opponent than are those played from the back of the court, and the shorter distance which the ball has to travel gives the opponent less time for his reply. It should be remembered too that downward hit volleys and smashes are more powerful than groundstrokes, so the opponent's racket work is put under pressure from the sheer pace of the ball.

By being positioned nearer to the net, he is reducing the shot options available to his opponent, as a greater part of the width of the court can be covered by the net player.

High trajectory, semi-defensive shots from the opponent which would become deep, and so challenging, shots from the baseline are welcomed by the net player, who can cut them off with aggressive high volleys.

The disadvantages

The net player has many opportunities of gaining an advantage or hitting an outright winner, but he has his problems as well.

Following a groundstroke in to the net can have its disadvantages if there is any weakness in the movement or stroke technique needed for the tactic. If you have a fear of being passed or lobbed, this can affect your confi-

Below: A wide-angled shot has put the player under pressure and his percentage option would be a high defensive lob.

dence, and consequently the effectiveness of the tactic. Like any tactic, using the approach shot to give yourself the opportunity of getting closer to the net is only useful if it is successful more often than not. Expect to be passed on some occasions, but practise the tactics involved so that this happens as rarely as possible.

Look for the challenge

In the earlier stages of your proficiency, you will probably feel much more secure playing at the back of the court than in the exposed areas nearer the net. When starting to develop an all-court game you may at first become disheartened when you make errors or if you are passed, or driven back by a lob. You may well lack the confidence, when facing an aggressive opponent, to take the opportunity of moving in to the net, and return to the safer, if less profitable, area at the back of the court.

Many players tell themselves, throughout their playing careers, that they simply do not like playing at the net. This is a pity, because all-court play can be very enjoyable as well as giving many more opportunities for successful and imaginative play.

Think of the number of times that you have seen a net player in doubles miss a couple of volleys, and then retreat to the baseline to be stationed alongside his serving partner. But think also of how much easier it is to play doubles against two back-court players than against two who are eager to play at the net as much as possible. The same applies in singles, where a defensively minded opponent will cause far fewer problems for you than one who uses surprise and aggression by moving to the net frequently to attack.

Certainly, at first, the inexperienced player may find that moving to the net may not pay as high dividends as staying back. Only by persistent practice, and trying to make net play an integral part of your match play will you progress to better results and greater

confidence. It is fun to hit winners from close to the net, and satisfying to realize that it is you who are calling the tune during the match, and that your opponent is feeling the effects of the pressures that you are putting on him!

Above: The players at the baseline are seizing the opportunity to move forward together as a team and try to set up a strong attacking position at the net.

Choose your approach shots

When making your approach shots, choose to play them against balls which land in the service courts, or in the area halfway between the service line and the baseline. One of the best opportunities for an approach shot is a weak service. Approach shots should be down-the-line more often than across court, as the latter opens up a wide net area through which you may be passed. However, approach across court if your opponent has moved wide to the other side of the court, or if he has a weaker forehand or backhand, giving you the chance to play a strong shot against it and force a weak reply from him.

Choose to use mainly the type of drive (lifted, topspin or slice) which you favour most, but vary the choice sometimes to break up your opponent's rhythm or because one type of drive is more suitable for controlling the ball you are playing.

Practising the approach shot

Practise for deep approach shots by setting yourself a target within three yards of the baseline (except occasionally when approaching behind an angled drive: then the acute angle requires your shot to land about service line length).

Do not aim too close to a sideline, as the risk of error is too great. About a yard from the sideline is a realistic target, even after much practice.

Play approach shots while still moving forward, checking your movement to short strides when near to the ball, so that you are balanced during the shot.

Pick up speed for a few longer strides towards the net and then check your stride to gain the best balance possible, ready to play your first volley. However, make sure that you are balanced so that you can move back quickly to position for a smash if the opponent chooses to play a lob.

Follow up the approach shot

If the return from your approach shot is high enough for you to attack with a high volley, play aggressively for a winner, but always be ready to move again to deal with a possible return. If

Below: The player has been lobbed and is sprinting backwards in order to play a smash or a recovery shot after the ball has bounced. Notice how he watches the ball carefully.

the return is low, then bend your knees to play a firm volley deep into your opponent's court. Get ready to move forward, and to either side, to play another volley, or back for a lob. You will need to give yourself as much time as possible for the next shot, only relaxing when you see that the ball has not been returned.

Much of the advice for approaching the net behind your service (see pages 50 and 51) also applies to moving in behind a groundstroke approach shot. The chance to move in comes when your opponent has offered you a ball which is short in length. The opportunity is certainly there if the shot lands in your service courts or a yard or so beyond the service line. As you improve at playing approach shots and gain in confidence, you should be able to play them off balls which land only a little nearer to the net than to the baseline. Top class players will move to the net behind shots which are played well back from the net, but progress in stages, starting with the very short ball.

Play deep approach shots

If your approach shot lands reasonably near to your opponent's baseline he is restricted in angles for a passing shot, while you have a long sight of the ball coming back to you, and time to position yourself for your volley or smash. If your approach is short, the advantage can pass to your opponent, as he has angles available to pass you, and there will be little time for you to prepare for your return. Do not stop when you play your approach shot, but check your balance and continue to move towards the net as you are playing your shot. Take short strides or skip steps as you are striking the ball, then pick up speed, with longer strides, as you move towards the net.

Check your balance again while preparing for your first volley, and be prepared to move back instead, in the event of your opponent lobbing. Place your first volley deep into your opponent's court and be ready to move in

again if there is a chance of playing a higher volley from very near to the net. Watch your opponent intently as he is playing his shot so you can read as soon as possible whether he is going to drive or lob and judge the direction of his shot.

There is less chance of being passed if you approach mainly down the line instead of across the court. But there are times when the cross-court approach is preferable, such as when your opponent has a weak side which should be attacked, or when he is out of position and you have a large gap to play your approach shot into.

Topspin or slice approach shots

Choose mainly the type of shot with which you are most confident. However, varying between topspin and slice can unsettle your opponent.

Slice is usually easier to play while you are on the move, and it also tends to produce a low bounce which may

bring a sharply lifted shot from your opponent, giving you a reasonably high ball to volley against.

Topspin approaches can give your opponent an awkward high bounce to deal with, but it is even more important to hit topspin approaches to good length as the short, high bouncing ball is easy for your opponent to attack.

Try the moonball as a variation of approach shot.

Play a very high trajectory approach shot off a longer length shot from your opponent, with some topspin, and deep into his court. Your ball will bounce high, and will have to be played by your opponent from his run-back. He will have a very little angle for his return and you will have plenty of time to position yourself for it. You should be ready to deal with a lob in this situation, as if you have played this shot well your opponent will have few other options.

Above: Billie Jean King, having followed her serve to the net, plays a difficult low volley, showing all the poise and balance that were the hallmarks of her game.

Playing the percentages

The success of any shot depends on its difficulty in relation to the standard of the player making it, and on how much he is attempting to achieve. If his shot is played against a ball which is putting him under pressure, and he tries to be very aggressive, then his return is likely to fail. The *percentage chance* of success would have risen if he had attempted to play a less adventurous shot.

It is just as important not to *miss* opportunities to attack by playing a too cautious return against an easy ball. Although the percentage chance of not making an error may be very high, there would be little or no pressure put on the opponent.

For these reasons attacking shots should be made with the amount of aggression which you judge to have a very reasonable chance of success. The degree of aggression should be related to your normal standard of play. If it is underestimated then a profitable chance has been missed, and if it is overestimated then the chance of success for the shot is less than it should be.

Adjust to the importance of the point

With a match point against you it is *vital* to make the opponent play the ball. If you do not return his shot then you have lost the match. So it is wise to play shots with a higher percentage chance of success, at the expense of aggression. Percentage shots should also be adjusted for set points, and for game points, when they are against you. The safety factor should be rather less than for match points, but it is still wise to take a little less risk when a mistake could lose you the game or even cost you the set.

On the other hand, when important points are in your favour, a little more risk is often worthwhile. Of course, one should not go for an outright winner if the chance of making it is slight, but a solid percentage shot puts pressure on an opponent who is at that stage unlikely to counter attack. If he is having to defend to stay in the match he may well give winning opportunities to his opposition if pressure is maintained against him. This leads on to another important rule.

Keep the opponent under pressure

If you have been making many errors through trying to do more than your skill allows, you should try to play a better percentage game and reduce your errors. Thus your opponent is not being given as many easy points. The pressure is on him to earn them!

Playing the percentages well is very

Below: A good example of the baseline player playing into the gap created by his previous shot. His percentage play in this instance must be to aim down the line.

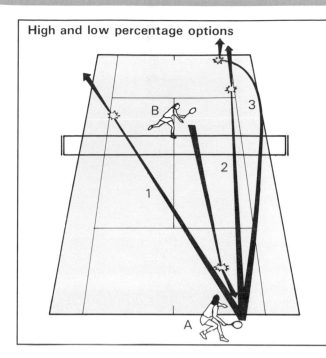

High and low percentage options

Left. In this diagram with the net player B having forced player A outside his baseline into the defensive zone, the low percentage option is for player A to hit a short-angled passing shot (1). The normal replies are a passing shot down the line (2) or a lob to the back court (3). The net player B may anticipate the normal percentage options and occasionally it is good tactics by player A to play the unexpected.

important on the serve and return of serve. Getting your first serve in, even at the expense of a little speed, is always a good tactic for important points. Equally, a solid rather than spectacular return of serve is always good percentage play in pressure situations.

When to risk a little more
At forty-love in your favour the percentage chance of success can be lowered to play a more than usually aggressive shot, or one at a small target. The extra risk involved is worthwhile as, if you do not win the point, there are still two more game points in your favour to come. However do not forget the advice given on pages 54 and 55: a steady opponent is still a force to be reckoned with even when he is behind!

Left: Kevin Curren plays a successful passing shot down the line against Boris Becker. Instead of playing a cross-court passing shot, he has obviously played the stronger percentage shot.

Court surfaces

One of the arts of being a good tennis competitor is to be able to adapt your game to various types of court surface. You will have to adjust to the height and pace of the ball as it bounces, and to the texture of the surface, which affects footwork.

The footwork required for playing on a hard surface with no top dressing is very different from that needed on one which has sand or loose grit on its surface. Grass and various types of carpet offer different footholds which affect braking and turning. Only experience of playing on a variety of surfaces will provide the knowledge you need as to the footwork variations required for each surface.

Speed of the court

There are fast surfaces on which the ball is slowed only a little by a contact with the ground, a number of inter-mediate surfaces, and slow surfaces where friction impedes the ball considerably. *Grass* and *smooth carpets* are fast. *Clay, macadam* and *damp shale* are slow surfaces. In between for pace are *artificial grass* (fast/medium), and *cement* (medium/slow), *painted hard* without a top dressing (medium and medium/slow depending on the make of court), and *matt carpet* (medium).

Fast surfaces provide opportunities for attack with the service and ground-strokes, while volleys and smashes can be put away with little hope of recovery by the opponent. So serve-

and-volleying, and getting to the net at other times, are good tactics. Drop shots are of less value while lobs must be deep and topspun when possible, as the shorter lob is a gift for the opponent.

Slow surfaces require more patience from the players. Winners are less

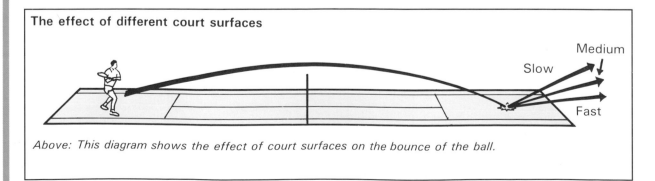

The effect of different court surfaces

Medium

Slow

Fast

Above: This diagram shows the effect of court surfaces on the bounce of the ball.

frequent because good attacking shots are slowed giving the opponent the chance to recover them. The service has less effect so spin services to good length should be used sometimes instead of always attempting outright aces. When approaching the net, you must be sure that your approach shot is deep. The opponent has time to position himself for a passing shot, so short approach shots will be of little value to the player who is trying to gain a commanding net position.

Beware of becoming too negative on a slow surface. Patient aggression is the best strategy. Prepare patiently for attacking opportunities and then do not waste them.

For other surfaces, with a pace somewhere between fast and slow, continue to use your strengths and cover your weaknesses, but play more of an all round game, with the mental approach between the bold attack which you use on fast surfaces and the patient aggression you adopt for slow surfaces. Think of such surfaces as giving you the advantages of both fast and slow courts, while offering your opponent the drawbacks of either kind of court.

Adapt to the ball's bounce

Comfortable hitting is the basis for all stroke making. Adjustments to the choice of shot have to be made according to the surface. For low bouncing courts it is wise to use slice more, while high bouncing surfaces offer chances for topspin attack. Get to the net on low bounce surfaces, as the opponent has to lift the ball. Play long length, high bouncing balls on surfaces which make the balls bounce even higher, and counteract this tactic, if your opponent is using it, by playing the early ball (see page 52): this will minimize the bounce he is trying to exploit.

Finally, try to gain as much experience as possible of playing on different court surfaces. This will help you to adapt to varying court conditions.

These are the three contrasting surfaces that all world-class players need to master: Far left above: A clay court surface (slow); Far left below: A cement court surface (medium fast); Above: A grass court (fast).

Using the elements

Too many players make sweeping statements like 'I cannot play if it is windy' or 'I'm useless if the sun gets into my eyes'. Such players are easy to conquer, as they have partly given up before the match has started. The best and most positive approach is to gain experience by practising in difficult conditions whenever the opportunity is available. The really effective competitor *welcomes* the pressure from difficult conditions or situations, as he knows that he will be less affected by them than many of his opponents.

Windy conditions
First, accept that you will not be able to play as well as usual if the wind or sun are troublesome. But neither will the opponent, so an important aspect of the match becomes the issue of who will be the least disturbed. In all types of wind, from behind you, in your face, or across the court, give yourself wider margins for error when aiming shots near to the lines.

To keep the ball in play in a high wind is even more important than usual, as every ball which lands in the opponent's court presents more problems for him than it does on a still day, and more opportunities for him to make mistakes.

Wind in your face
If the wind is blowing in your face, then you can generally afford to hit higher over the net, aiming for a deeper length than normal.
● Use sliced drives for penetration against it.
● Keep your returns low against a volleyer; hitting up with the wind behind him, he may hit out over the baseline.
● Play drop shots more frequently than usual.
● If you lob, do so very aggressively with topspin. The wind will help keep the ball in, while it will make the ball's

flight difficult for your opponent to judge.
● Use spin services, as the pace of flatter ones will be reduced. Make it your policy to get the first serve in, controlling it with spin.

Wind behind
If the wind is blowing from behind you, then you should hit lower over the net. Do not aim your shots as deep as usual.
● Use topspin drives to keep the ball in court.
● Get to the net as much as possible, as it will be difficult to pass you.
● Do not use the drop-shot: lob only occasionally, and then with topspin.
● Allow for the effect of the wind on the length of all your shots, and it will help you by adding to their pace.

Wind across the court
In cross winds the following will help
● When playing to the side from which the wind is coming, aim close to the line.
● When aiming to the other side aim well into court from the line.
● Sliced services to the deuce court, and topspin services to the advantage court, will have added effect if served to the side *towards* which the wind is

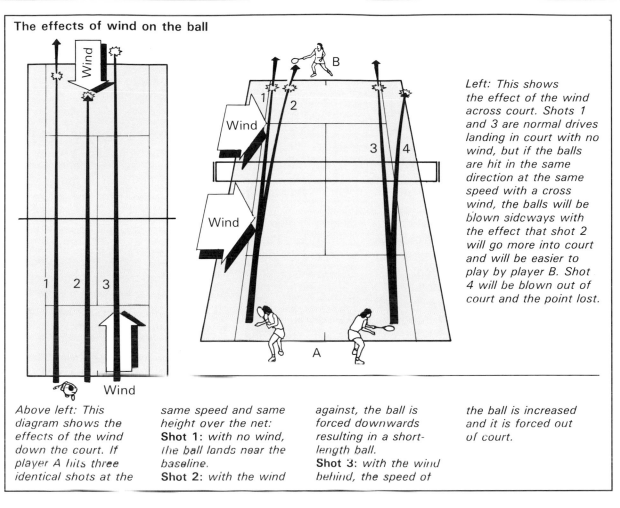

The effects of wind on the ball

Wind

1   2

Wind

Wind

B

1   2

3   4

A

Wind

Left: This shows the effect of the wind across court. Shots 1 and 3 are normal drives landing in court with no wind, but if the balls are hit in the same direction at the same speed with a cross wind, the balls will be blown sideways with the effect that shot 2 will go more into court and will be easier to play by player B. Shot 4 will be blown out of court and the point lost.

Above left: This diagram shows the effects of the wind down the court. If player A hits three identical shots at the *same speed and same height over the net:* **Shot 1:** *with no wind, the ball lands near the baseline.* **Shot 2:** *with the wind* *against, the ball is forced downwards resulting in a short-length ball.* **Shot 3:** *with the wind behind, the speed of* *the ball is increased and it is forced out of court.*

blowing. Take a similar policy with short length angled shots.

Beat the sun

There are a number of things to practise doing if the sunlight is bothering you. Experiment with the use of an eyeshade or a light cap, or other headgear which can protect your eyes from glare. If this helps you, and the sartorial effect gives you confidence, then your problem is solved. Otherwise, try closing, or nearly closing one eye, or partially closing both eyes, especially when serving. Serving with the sun in your eyes is particularly difficult, so practise this whenever you can.

Getting the first service in, even at the expense of some pace, is a sensible tactic as this way you can avoid a double dose of peering at the ball against its very bright light. Letting very high lobs bounce is also wise, or your eyes will be turned up for a long time to watch the falling ball before you hit it. Between points give your eyes a rest by glancing briefly into the darker areas of the court. In doubles with a right and left handed pair, choose the ends to serve from which better suits each player.

Use the sun

Lobbing into the sun creates difficulties for your opponent. If this is done persistently your opponent may be discouraged from coming to the net, which would give you a distinct tactical advantage. When used in doubles to drive opponents back from the net, lob over the player who is more affected by the sun. High bouncing drives and 'moonballs' as variations from normal rallying are made even more effective if your opponent is facing the sun.

Be flexible during a point

We have spoken about the similarities, in certain areas, between chess and tennis. In chess it is common for one player to feel quite confident that his attacking play will lead to checkmate in two or three moves, but for his opponent quietly to move a piece and himself call 'checkmate'. The attacking player made the fatal mistake of being so immersed with the part of the board in which he was attacking that he had overlooked an equally good attack from his opponent from another direction!

Tennis players can fall into a similar trap. As you attack, be very aware of what countering moves your opponent may be making to turn his defensive role into an attacking one. Overlook even one possible counter move and you are likely to lose the point because you are not prepared.

Be prepared to change your tactics

In tennis you do not have as much time to think as you have in chess, so keep your mind alert, cool and concentrating. A fine approach shot may have sent your opponent deep into the back corner of his court but, desperately perhaps, he hoists a vicious topspin lob. You, savouring the winning volley before it has happened, are left stranded. Take nothing for granted, and be as prepared as possible for any eventuality including, or perhaps especially, the unexpected ones.

You must be equally alert and flexible in your mind, to take the sudden chance for an attack for which you could not have planned. You may be rallying with the intention of wrongfooting your opponent as soon as he starts to race, too soon, to cover the vacant side of his court, giving you the chance to play the ball back to the area he has just left.

But what if, instead of this happening, he hits a poor shot without as much length as he intended? Be ready to forget immediately about your intended tactic. Take the opportunity to move in and play a solid approach shot, and dominate the net.

Be ready for his counter attack

You may be moving in behind a well played shot to his backhand, expecting to volley or smash his return across court. But what if he hits a fast low shot, wider from you than expected? Change your plan, as if you now volley across court you cannot, under pressure, hit a shot good enough to trouble him. He would beat you because there is a wide gap for him to drive into, off a fairly easy ball. So be flexible enough to change to playing the ball back, safely and with less power, to his backhand. By doing this, you are still in the point instead of having given it away by being inflexible.

Change your plan, then, in the middle of a point if an unexpected opportunity occurs for you, or if the situation suddenly becomes more difficult for you and you have to change from aggressive play to defensive play to stay in the point.

Practise to react quickly to the unexpected

It is important to gain experience in dealing with unexpected returns from an alert opponent. One way of doing this is to play as much as possible against more experienced players. They will offer you a variety of responses to your tactics and plenty of opportunity to experiment in dealing with them and thinking ahead, quickly and flexibly.

A net-cord or a bad bounce are other happenings which you cannot forecast, and there is no way of practising for these. You must develop your instinct and reactions to deal with these situations. All types of reflex practices, including volleying in pairs against a practice partner standing near to you, will help you to learn how to react to the unexpected.

Opposite: Miloslav Mecir whose distinct and unique strategies have confused and upset a myriad of opponents.

Use spin as a tactic

Spin causes the ball to behave in a different way to when it is hit flat. Topspin, whether in a service or in groundstrokes, causes the ball to bounce higher and apparently pick up speed after it has bounced. Slice slows the ball through the air and makes it bounce lower than when struck flat or with topspin. It follows that a variation of flat, topspin and slice shots can confuse the opponent, and upset his timing because of the different speeds of the shots and the difference in height of the bounces. For these reasons, a random pattern of spin variations can be a useful tactic for serving and for rallying.

The moonball

Topspin drives can be used tactically by varying the height over the net, and their length. A very high drive, often called a moonball, in between lower trajectory shots can upset your opponent's rhythm, because it needs a very different type of return. The moonball is also a good tactical shot when you need time to reposition yourself in the court. Play it deep, with plenty of topspin to make the bounce awkward to control.

Sliced shots

Slice, when serving or used in an approach shot, is a good shot behind which to move in towards the net. Its low bounce makes the opponent lift the ball sharply, giving you the opportunity to volley the still-rising ball.

Slice can also be used to get yourself out of trouble. When you have to play a shot while slightly off balance,

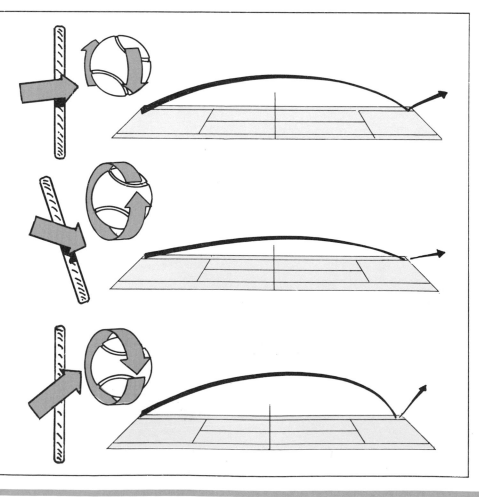

The effects of spin
These diagrams show the effects of spin on the ball.

Flat stroke
Right: A flat stroke has an even trajectory and a regular bounce.

Slice stroke
Right: A slice stroke will carry further and generally bounce lower.

Topspin stroke
Right: A topspin stroke dips at the end of its flight and bounces sharply forwards and upwards.

or when you are too cramped or stretched, use slice. It is easier to control than topspin when you are under pressure.

Topspin

Topspin causes the ball to dip towards the end of its flight. So use it against the net player, whether he is in place or moving in, as the low dipping ball will put pressure on his volley. He is almost sure to have to play defensively if you have aimed well and managed to keep the ball over the net as it dips.

A useful variation for topspin is to use it in sharply angled returns off short widely angled shots from your opponent. Using strong lift, particularly on the forehand side, apply a lot of topspin and hit round the side of the ball. Aim for the ball to land short of the service line, running well out of the court. On the backhand side using slice is often a preferable way of gaining the same angle, but with less penetration.

Countering spin

While the intelligent use of spin will improve the effectiveness of many of your own shots, it is clearly important to read the flight and bounce of your opponent's ball and judge the effects of *his* spin tactics. Everything which has been said about the effects of spin from the point of view of your play will apply equally to his, so anticipate accordingly and position yourself to be able to deal with spin shots in the light of your own skill and experience.

Left: A good example of the set-up for the slice backhand. The player is just beginning his forward swing and is about to hit underneath the ball using backspin for greater control and accuracy.

Chapter 5 **Doubles**

Basic tactics for doubles

In doubles, all the same principles regarding stroke play, tactical and strategic play and psychological awareness apply as in the singles game. However the doubles game introduces additional elements which can turn it into a very different experience, with advantages and disadvantages when compared to singles.

The fact that there are four players on the court, even though the court area is a little larger, means that there are fewer gaps and more restricted angles for every stroke made, except the serve itself. But having four players means having four different personalities, each with their individual strengths and weaknesses. Unless a doubles pair are playing in perfect harmony, as one team (and this is very difficult to achieve and sustain) there will be more opportunities for exploiting weak strokes and variations in movement, for example, than are encountered in a singles match.

Learn the basic tactical principles listed below, and discuss them with your doubles partner so that you know each other's mind before you go onto the court. And watch top doubles players in action. At its best doubles, whether men's, women's or mixed, is a highly exciting game which makes great demands on the players' reactions. Fast and furious volleying at the net is common, and the art of keeping the ball in play is at its most refined, with sustained rallies and inspired stroke play frequently seen.

● Be familiar with the basic positions on court (see pages 76/77).
● Play as a team (see pages 78/79).
● Get nearer to the net than your opponents, so you can volley down, while they are forced to volley up.
● Keep the ball low over the net.
● Attack the weaker opponent.
● Win your service games.

Get nearer to the net
The downward hit volleys off higher balls are more often winners than the low volley, which cannot be struck as hard with safety. So if all four players are near to the net each should keep the ball low over the net until one has the chance to move forward to meet a return when it is still higher than the net. This downward volley should be placed firmly for a winner.

Keep the ball low
To prevent the opponents from having opportunities to volley down, keep the ball low over the net with your groundstrokes and low volleys, forcing the opponents into a difficult defensive position. This is a good tactic for establishing yourself in a strong attacking net position.

Attack on the weaker side
This is an obvious tactic which is sometimes overlooked. It is occasionally better not to play on the stronger opponent, even though the tactical situation demands it, as a less tactically sound shot to the weaker opponent may be more profitable.

Nearly always lob over the weaker player. However, do not overdo the tactic of playing on the weaker opponent, as you may well disrupt your own game plan and give him enough warning and practice for his performance to improve rather than suffer!

Look for individual weaknesses in both players so that you can exploit them to your advantage.

Keeping the serving advantage
The advantage in doubles is strongly in favour of the serving team, so make every effort to hold your service games regularly. If you never drop a service game you cannot lose a match except through losing tie-breaks. Winning your service games gives you the overall confidence to go for the necesary break of the opponent's service, and can ease away the tension of being on the defensive.

Opposite: Although all four players are in attacking positions, the players in the foreground are nearer to the net and have a strong opportunity to hit the ball downwards, either into the gap or at the feet of their opponents.

Doubles – basic court positions

The server should be based half-way between the centre line and the doubles sideline. From that position he should be able to cover wide returns in the tramlines. If he is staying back after his service, he should take a ready position close to the baseline, again half-way between the centre and sidelines. If he follows his service in towards the net he should move straight ahead into the court, or swerve about a yard towards the sidelines, not follow the path of the service as he would in singles play. This straight ahead path to the net helps him to cover the cross court return from the receiver, while if the latter is returning at a sharp angle, then the little swerve covers the wider return.

The receiver takes the same base as for singles, adjusting forwards or backwards depending on the expected strength of the service, and of course moving in for the second service. He should also adjust his position laterally, to allow for the server's positioning and also for the anticipated angle of the ball.

The server's partner should be based about a yard inside the singles side-line, and about two yards from the net. His challenge is to cut off the receiver's returns. As his anticipation, movement and volleying improve, he should position himself nearer to the centre of the court, about two yards inside the singles service line and another yard back from the net. Once there he has a better chance of recovering for the deep lobs, but he must be alert enough to move forward to volley, from near to the net, instead of waiting for the ball to come through to him at his base.

The receiver's partner should be based on the service line about half-way between the sideline and the centre line. He should be very alert, and watching the opposing net player, in case he intercepts the receiver's return. If this happens, then a reflex counter volley from the receiver's partner is made easier by reading the body and racket movement of the server's partner. In doubles, quick reactions are very important, and this type of anticipation can help you to win many points.

If the receiver returns the ball past the net opponent to the server, then

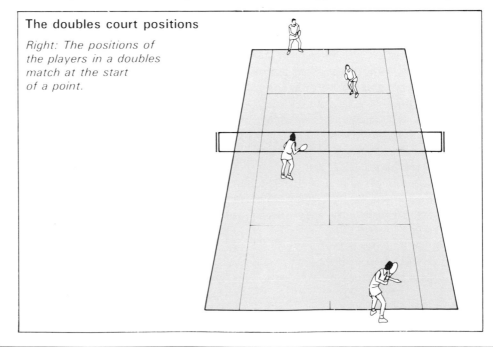

The doubles court positions

Right: The positions of the players in a doubles match at the start of a point.

Left: This shows basic court positions in doubles play. The server is about to serve his first serve and the receiver is waiting just outside the baseline. The service partner is in a strong net position with the receiver's partner standing temporarily in the mid-court area.
Below left: The server has just served to the advantage court (left) and is now moving in to play his first volley. He will subsequently follow into the net to develop a sound attacking position with his partner.

the receiver's partner should move forward to a more attacking position, from where he will hope to intercept the next shot from the server. By moving towards the net he also forces the server's partner to move back to a defensive position to cover his side of the court.

Get to the net as often as possible

In top class doubles a considerable percentage of points are won by volleys, so try to develop your game to include serve-and-volleying and moving to the net behind service returns whenever practicable, and play a valuable volleying role when you are the partner of either the server or the receiver. Good basic positions in court are an essential foundation for achieving these goals.

See the following pages for further advice on re-positioning after the opening shots of a point.

Play doubles as a team

Talk to your partner

It is invaluable when playing doubles to have good understanding with your partner. Be encouraging at all times. Supportive comments such as 'Good shot!' and 'Well tried!' are helpful to boost your partner's confidence. But not too many condolences, or he will think that *you* think he is playing badly! Remember that you are a team and it will not help if you start to blame each other for lost points. Be positive and supportive to each other, especially when the match becomes tense: a tight match often hinges on a small number of important points.

Plan together

Discuss game plans and tactics as you change ends, encouraging the feeling that you are members of a team, playing with immense enjoyment and hope at all times. If you have a regular partner then practise together, and plan for your matches. After them, and when the dust has settled, with the euphoria of a win or the disappointment of a loss no longer clouding your judgment, have an inquest. This is when you can prepare to repeat point-winning strengths, and try to eliminate costly weaknesses, ready for your next match.

● If your partner is forced wide, move a little towards his side of the court, to close some of the gap between you: never let the opponents hit a winner between you down the middle of the court.

● If he is at the net, join him there as soon as you have a reasonable opportunity to do so.

● If you are both at the net and one of you is forced back by a lob, the other should move back as well to create a sound defensive position at the back of the court.

● Position yourself to make the opponent play the ball wide down the lines, giving a greater chance that the ball will be hit out of court.

Call decisively

For balls which either player might play, call loudly 'Mine!' or 'Yours!'. Both players must abide by the decision of the first one to call. The slightest hesitation can be fatal, resulting in the ball going through unplayed. The player not accepting the shot can often read better whether or not the ball would be in or out. A decisive 'leave it' can be very helpful, but only if the call is made before your partner is committed to his shot. If the opponent's shot is a lob and it is doubtful whether the ball would land in or not, then a warning call of 'Bounce it!' gives your partner

Below: An excellent example of team work by all four players — the ball is moving across court to the right and both teams are moving sideways simultaneously to cover for the next shot.

the chance to go back and cover the lob. If the call is correct you have won the point, while if it lands in court there is still time to play the ball after it has bounced and your partner will have moved into position.

Create chances for each other
In any partnership, it does not matter which player hits the winning shot. Both players should work together to create oportunities for each other.

Two examples out of several opportunities which might arise to play as a team can be considered:
● A good service or return will often give your partner the chance for a winning volley from close to the net.
● A crisp low volley from just inside the service line can lead to an upward volley from an opponent. This may be the chance for your partner, nearer to the net, to intercept and play a winning volley.

Above: John McEnroe and Peter Fleming show superb synchronization of movement in moving backwards to cover a difficult lob.

Serving in doubles

The advice given in pages 46 and 47 on tactical serving in singles applies equally to doubles, but the following adjustments should be made.

In doubles the server has much less court area to cover to reach possible returns than he has in singles. In order to cover his side of the doubles court, with his partner covering the other side, he should serve from half-way between the centre line and the doubles sideline. From there he can cover cross court returns which are directed towards the tramlines, while having returns down the centre of the court, which his partner has not intercepted, within reasonable reach.

Study the section on serve-and-volleying on pages 50 and 51. It is worth underlining the advantages gained from getting the first service into court. By getting the first service in you can rob the receiver of the boost to his confidence which he gains from having to deal with a less dangerous second service. Nor does he have the opportunity to move in to threaten the normally weaker second service. The aim of increasing the percentage of successful first services is just as important in doubles as it is in singles

and it increases the confidence of both the server and his partner. Try for a good length, even at the expense of some pace. A good length service cuts down the possible angles of return, gives the server a longer sight of the return, and more time to move in towards the net.

Planning the service
When deciding where to serve to, and what type of service to use consider the following points:

● Play to the weaker side of the receiver, just as in singles.

● Serving down the middle of the court cuts down the angles of return which are available to the receiver, and gives the server's partner a better chance of intercepting.

● As a variation, slice wide to the deuce court receiver, and topspin wide to the advantage court. As the server's partner sees the receiver moving wide to return he must be sure to guard his sidelines which have become vulnerable to a down-the-line return.

● A spin service is slower through the air than a flat one. So it can be a good tactic sometimes to use a slice or topspin service for your first delivery,

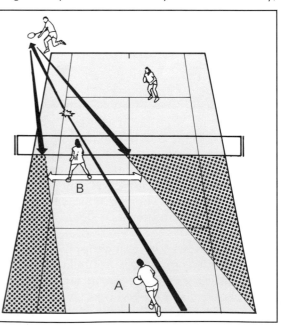

The angled serve

Right: This diagram shows the possible areas of return for the receiver when the server has served to a wide angle. Player B should be able to cover the unshaded area with one quick movement.

Left: The server is serving to the receiver's forehand, and the server's partner at the net must guard against leaving too big a gap down his lines.

giving you some more time to get further in towards the net.

● Vary your serve, both first and second. Unsettle the opponent by varying your speed, direction and spin. Do not let him settle into a predictable rhythm on his return.

● Try to communicate with your partner in advance of serving so that he is aware of any new tactics. This will enable him to take advantage of the situation from the net position.

These considerations are suggestions for good tactical serving in doubles. Do not concentrate on one only in your matches, but vary them to prevent the receiver from reading your intentions.

The deep serve

Right: This diagram shows the possible areas of return for the receiver when the server has served to a good length down the middle. Player B at the net should with one quick movement be able to cover the unshaded area.

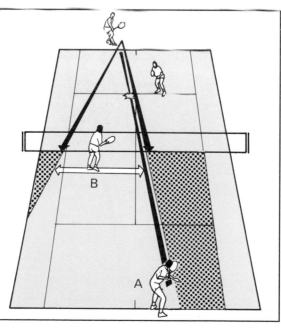

Returning the serve in doubles

The opening formation in doubles gives a decided advantage to the serving team, because the serving pair have the ball in their possession and can play the opening shot of the point at a speed and direction they decide, and with any spin they wish.

A good service can be hit harder than an equally good groundstroke. The server's partner has the chance of playing the first volley of a point, while he is based in a more aggressive position than the receiver's partner.

To counter these advantages the return of service can attempt to do one of several things:
● Neutralize the power of the service.
● Prevent the server's partner from intercepting.
● Pass the incoming server, or give him a difficult ball to volley.
● Lob to disrupt the opponents' formation.

Thus a sound service return, well placed tactically, can take the initiative from the serving team. Service returns must be rated as the second most important aspect of good doubles play, after serving. It is well worth discussing with your partner the policy to be followed for receiving, and incorporating it in your game plan.

Prepare for your returns
● Decide where it is best to be based for each return, using your knowledge of the opponent's method of serving. Vary this base as you begin to read his intentions, and to disrupt the server's rhythm.
● Settle down into an alert readiness position.
● Anticipate where the server is likely to aim. Will it be to your forehand or backhand or straight at you? Does he serve in a pattern, first to one side and

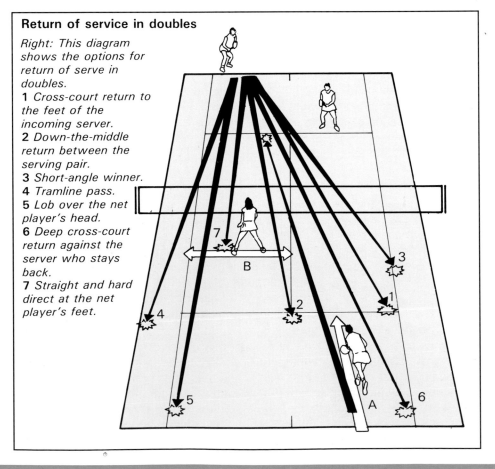

Return of service in doubles

Right: This diagram shows the options for return of serve in doubles.
1 Cross-court return to the feet of the incoming server.
2 Down-the-middle return between the serving pair.
3 Short-angle winner.
4 Tramline pass.
5 Lob over the net player's head.
6 Deep cross-court return against the server who stays back.
7 Straight and hard direct at the net player's feet.

then to the other? If his pattern is much more random, then try to out guess his intention.

● Read the flight of the ball as soon as it leaves the server's racket, while preparing quickly for the return.

Attacking returns

If the service offers little threat because it is short of length or medium paced, then attack it with your normal drive. There are several possibilities from which to choose:

● A pass towards the far sidelines.

● A low hard drive straight to the incoming server's feet.

● A drive down the centre, between the opponents.

● An attack down the server's partner's sidelines, either to pass him if he has moved across too soon, to catch him off guard, or even to warn him *not* to move across too early.

If the service is a strong one, and you still decide to attack, choose from the above options, but adjust your technique by shortening your racket take-back. You will not have time to complete your normal take-back and still make an effective shot.

Safety returns

It is generally unwise to attack when you are under pressure, but you should still try to play a firm, if less adventurous, shot. Do not use the drive between the opponents, but the other options can still worry them even though you are playing at a slower pace, perhaps using slice for a safer shot. The lob becomes a good alternative in a defensive situation like this.

Under extreme pressure be content mainly to block back your return or to lob high and defensively. Make every effort to return the ball so that your opponents have to play it again.

In general you will find that as the opponents' strength of serving, and the pressure they are bringing to bear, is increased, your shot options will decrease. If you can block the ball back defensively to the incoming server's feet you may force him to play

a difficult low volley, opening up an opportunity for your partner to intercept. The alternative strategy is to hit a high, deep lob which will enable your partner to to move back and join you in a solid defence position at the baseline.

Just occasionally, it may pay you to surprise your opponents by gambling everything on a counter attack. But do this as a last resort, not as a habit!

If the server stays back, move towards the net after making your return, which should be a long one, while your partner should close in a little so that you are dominating the net as a team.

Above: In this sequence, the left handed receiver has moved in to play a controlled slice backhand return, intending to force the server to play a difficult low volley.

Interception

Dominating the net

When two opponents are defending from the back of their court it is difficult to win points if your team also stays back. Imagine a game with all four players starting at the back of their court and staying there during a point. The rallies could be very long and difficult to win, as all the players have a smaller area to cover than in singles play, and the likelihood of errors occurring will be greatly reduced.

Now imagine a game in which two players are stationed near to the net and their opponents are based at the back of their court. The net players have a great advantage as they can use angled volleys and stop volleys, while their downward hits, from above the height of the net are more powerful than their opponents' groundstrokes, which will generally have to be hit *upwards* to clear the net.

Each team should have the intention of being the first to volley. The serving team has the initiative providing the server moves to the net after his service. If he does, then when the server's partner cannot intercept, the first shot from their team will either be a volley, or a smash.

If, however, the server stays back, the initiative passes to the receiving team unless the server's partner can intercept. So the receiver should move in when that is practicable to consolidate his team's net position. He will obviously be hard pressed to do so if the service has put him under pressure, but if the service is short of length then the receiver should play his return and move in behind it.

Volleying down

When all four players in a doubles game are near the net, volleying against each other, look for the opportunity to close in very quickly to meet a ball while it is still above the net height. Punch it down firmly between the opponents, or at the feet of one of them. When it is an easy shot and you have the time, aim to play it wide towards the sidelines. Remember to use the lob volley sometimes to drive the opponents back from the net. As soon as you see that a smash is not possible, hold your ground and close into the net, as you will have a strong attacking position. If the lob volley is short, and a smash is possible for the other team, then move back as quickly as possible ready to defend against it.

Interceptions

Double play offers two main opportunities for intercepting the ball:
● When the server's partner has seen

Right: This example shows how two players can dominate the net and out-manoeuvre the defending team. The player in the tramlines has been forced out of position and his partner on the baseline must now temporarily cover the whole court until they recover their correct positions.

Doubles net play

Right: In this diagram, pair A have established a strong team position at the net whilst pair B are in a weak position because one player is stranded on the service line. This is a good opportunity for team A to volley downwards at the feet of the player in mid-court (1), or into the gap between the two players (2).

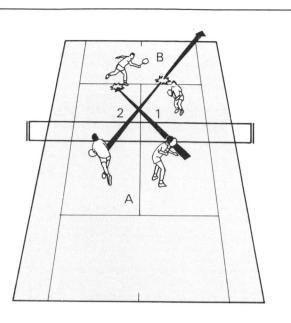

that the receiver is in a weak position, he may move across and intercept the cross court return of service.

● When the receiver's partner has seen that the server, who is coming in to the net, is having to play a low, defensive first volley. He may now move across to intercept the volley's cross–court shot.

Either of these two interceptions, used intelligently, can have the effect of making your opponents undecided and so can affect their performance. If this tactic is being used *against* you, do not panic, but concentrate more carefully on the ball and make up your mind quickly as to which shots you are going to play. Be positive!

Below: In this doubles match at Wimbledon, Chris Lewis, with the headband at the net, has intercepted John McEnroe's return, hitting the ball for a winner. Notice how his partner is moving across behind him to cover the area he has left free.

Chapter 6 **Practise to Improve**

Planned practice

If your highest ambition is to play a pleasant social game several times a year, but not as your main recreation, you do not need a fitness trainer, a coach or a sports psychologist! However you will still get more enjoyment and confidence from tennis if you practise the main strokes, develop a few tactics, get a little fitter and get into the habit of positive thinking. Your game will improve and you will be able to reproduce your practice 'form' in your matches. As you improve you may decide to raise your ambition, play more frequently, and so enjoy the game more.

If you want to make a determined effort to become a high level player your practice in the areas of stroke play, tactics, fitness and temperament must be of consistently high quality.

Aim between the extremes

People play tennis at every conceivable level of proficiency, from the purely recreational, to club level, to regional tournament level, up to national standard and, finally, international playing standard. Each of these subdivisions can be divided further. Some clubs are stronger than others, and one country seems to dominate the international game at one particular time.

Practices are of two types

Repetitive practices, or drills, are the basic types of practice, in which attention is paid to aim, consistency and power of hitting, as required.

The second type of practice is practising in situations, and it relates directly to matchplay. Here, attention is given to practising specific match situations – returning the serve, for example – in order to get the player used to reacting to the situation on court and playing the shots he has learnt in context.

Your practices should include both these types. If you take tennis lessons, your coach will arrange your sessions to include a mixture of different types of practice, to suit your needs.

Drills

For many tennis players a practice session involves rallying down the middle of the court, a few volleys and overheads and then an actual set or matchplay. They generally neglect the area which is probably the best method of self-improvement – practising disciplined drills.

Drilling is the key to improvement and is essential in the development of any player. Improvement comes from repetitive practice of one or more aspects of matchplay in a controlled situation free from the pressures of competition. This form of training aims to stimulate players' interest and direct them towards improving and developing specific aspects of their game.

Relating drills to matchplay

In all forms of tennis coaching and training, work should always relate to matchplay situations. It is of little use being a technically competent player who in matchplay continually chooses the wrong options either through ignorance or indiscipline. The use of drills can help a player acquire new dimensions to his game. This can be achieved by practising very simple tactical situations repetitively, then gradually increasing the pressure in a variety of ways, such as speed, width,

linking two or three shots, counting errors and winners, playing a *loaded* game (with extra penalties or awards for certain aspects) and finally, playing a proper game.

Feeding

The correct level of feeding is fundamental to the success of any drill. It may be necessary for the coach to instruct players on how and where to feed and often to act personally as the feeder. When the coach is trying to construct a rally from single ball feeding, the timing of the feed is important. The coach should hit the feed ball as the previous shot goes past him or her, in order to create a rally effect.

The feeders should also regularly change the position from where they are feeding in order to create realistic and varied angles of play. They should also regularly change the speed, flight and spin of the feed ball to relate to normal match situations.

When committed tennis players are practising amongst themselves without a coach, then sympathetic feeding of the ball and vocal encouragement can make all the difference between the success or failure of any tennis training session.

Good feeding should help develop a player's rhythm and 'groove' and subsequently put him into much more demanding situations relating to matchplay conditions.

Above: In this practice, known as 'Threes', the two players at the net are moving the single player around the singles court and thus putting him under varying degrees of pressure.

Opposite: In order to achieve a grooved or consistent method of play as shown here, the successful player needs to allocate a considerable amount of time to effective practice.

Practising effectively

There is a bridge to cross between practising and playing in a match. Players who perform well in isolated repetitive drills may not be good match players. In matches shots are played in often unpredictable patterns; first a service, then perhaps a volley or a smash, followed by another volley, or a groundstroke. Or the pattern could be a backhand return of service, followed by a forehand, another backhand, then a volley and, perhaps, a smash. You have to be able to turn from one skill to another quickly and, sometimes, unexpectedly. If practice has only been done in drills, in which the same type of shot is played repetitively, the transfer to matchplay is a very difficult one.

The best method of practising is to alternate between repetitive drills, which can improve technique, accuracy and concentration, and then move on to practising parts of matchplay (known as situation practices) such as playing an approach shot followed by volleys. This recreates a part of a specific match situation.

You can 'win' in practice but lose the match

Why is it that frequently a player looks impressive in the practice before a match, but is far less effective when the match begins? Practice only shows his stroke play efficiency against balls which are directed near to him, while his service warm up is aimed into an empty court. The practice therefore shows little of his speed about the court, none of his tactical ability, and very little of his mental attributes or deficiencies. He may concentrate well or badly, but the onlooker, or opponent, has no clues from the practice as to his determination, confidence, tactical strategy or his physical ability, all of which contribute to the effectiveness of a match player.

The underlying needs

The strokes which you demonstrate in the practice, can be likened to the tip of an iceberg, which is for all to see above the water. As the match progresses, fitness and tactics will also be revealed, but what is under the water can never be seen clearly. There lie the driving forces behind performance; the mental approaches that drive on the competitor, or cause him to falter under the rapidly changing pressures of matchplay. René Lacoste, the famous French Davis Cup Player called these mental approaches the *impondérables* as they can never be measured accurately.

Below: Michael Chang's progress to the top has been achieved by a thorough and scientific approach to all areas of tennis, but especially in relation to his practice and training.

1 2

Left: For many players the service action is probably the most difficult in tennis. Simple throwing exercises with a tennis ball are ideal for developing the throwing action of the serve.

How deep lies the will to win, how much frustration can a player take before giving in to it, how far can self-control be tested before it breaks? How much do the *impondérables* contribute to performance? They cannot be measured, but matches are won or lost because of them.

Practise your strokes, but also work to improve your fitness, strategy and tactics, and the contribution to competition of your attitude of mind.

The top players in world tennis are those with *sound strokes*, who use them well in *strategy and tactics*, are superbly *fit* and have the *mental* strengths to produce their performance under pressure. However far you want to progress in the game, you should consider all four areas and not rely on good technical strokes alone. You should choose practices that contribute to them all.

Develop the art of practising in all four areas in order to ensure you maxi- mize your performance capabilities. There are chapters on all four areas. The objective is to marry the four areas together through practice and the experience of matchplay.

Enjoy practising

Finally, remember that tennis is a game to be enjoyed, and you will not enjoy playing in a match if you do not enjoy the practice as well. One way of obtaining a sense of achievement is to measure the progress that you are making: it is easy to feel the difference as your hitting becomes smoother and firmer, your accuracy can be measured by using targets, and improvements in your general fitness will be felt in every area of your life! Do not overdo prac- tice, or go on until you are exhausted, but leave off while you are still alert enough to play your shots well. If you go on trying to perfect a technique or a tactic after you have become really tired, it will become worse, not better.

Basic drills

A drill is a repetitive practice specifically aimed at improving a selected aspect of your game. The quality of a practice is more important than its length, so concentrate on the best shots of which you are capable at the time of the practice, playing them for consistency and firmness of stroke.

Cross-court driving

Hit drives across court from the deuce courts. Each player should return to the centre of his baseline between strokes, before moving off again to play his next shot. Targets should be used to develop accuracy and aid concentration. A racket head cover placed at the centre of the target area, is one example of a readily available and easily moved marker.

As you progress, two targets can be placed, one for long and the other for short-length angles in your practice. The hitter can aim at each target in turn, or make an early decision as to his choice of target. Every shot must be struck with a definite purpose, while good quality, relative to standard of play, must be maintained.

Tramline rallying

Straight driving (for passing shots, or down the line rallying shots) is a challenging practice when played up and down the tramlines, where there is a ready-made target. Driving up and down the centre of the court can permit careless aiming, as shots wide of the intended area can still be in the court. The tramlines give a precise target. To progress, aim each shot at first beyond the service line, and later beyond a marker placed at the side of the doubles sideline. Start with forehands, change to backhands, then play forehand and backhand shots alternately to exercise your footwork.

To score, count one for each ball that lands in the tramlines during a rally. The ball can bounce outside of the tramlines, but the rally ends if the ball hits the net, bounces twice or is over the baseline. Volleying to keep the ball in play is not allowed!

Below: These two players are practising cross-court driving, aiming to play the ball deep into the back section of the court. This practice can be used in the first instance as a simple technique practice. As the players improve, they should practise their recovery to the ready position on the baseline.

Long-length rallies

These are excellent for improving concentration as well as for footwork and stroke production. Rally to place every ball in the oblong at the back of the court between the baseline, service line and two single sidelines. Use good firm shots, as patting or pushing the ball in will be of no benefit. Attempt to increase your personal record of the longest rally, keeping the ball bouncing in the prescribed area.

This drill can be adapted to your level of experience. At first, keep the ball directed to the centre of the court, giving you a large target. As your standard improves increase the target area towards the sidelines so that you are practising movement and footwork as well as stroke play. At the higher levels of ability, this basic drill is very good as a training exercise as well as an excellent test of skill, accuracy and concentration.

Top: This shows tramline rallying. The two players behind the tramline are hitting consistently keeping the ball bouncing within the tramlines.
Above: This example shows backhand cross-court ralleys for length. The players are playing backhand to backhand, hitting for length.

Drills for volleys

One player 'feeds' with groundstrokes, and the other volleys. Change roles after each ten minutes. There are numerous variations on this basic exercise, so adjust the speed of feeding and the challenge to the volleyer according to the requirements of your practice session, and the standard of the players.

Initially, the volleyer can practise high forehand volleys from a distance of about two yards from the net as his base. Progress to high backhand volleys, and then to the low volleys, moving back for the latter to about a yard inside the service line.

Mix high and low volleys
The feeder sends balls to either side of the volleyer, alternately at first, then at random, varying the height of his drives. In this way, 'reading' the ball becomes very important, as does returning to the readiness position after each shot.

To provide variety and competition use targets to direct the volley, and feed from different areas of the court. The feeder can vary the pace as well as the height of the ball, and drive to either side of the volleyer at increasing distances. Score, and compete against your practice partner by counting the number of consecutive successful volleys, as well as the number of hits on the target.

Volleying in pairs
Both players move to about two yards inside the service lines. Vary this by staggering the bases so that volleys are angled to the left and then to the right. Then vary the distances from the net of the bases, moving nearer to the net to speed reactions, and further from it to practise long low volleys.

Score as a team by trying for as long a rally as you can achieve and try to improve on your record. Maintain the quality of the shots. Compete by playing more aggressively but in a restricted area, such as between the centre line and the singles sideline, and score one point for each time the opponent makes an error.

Lob-and-smash
Use similar sequences for practising the lob-and-smash. Start with non-

Right: A practice to develop control and reflexes with both players in semi-attacking positions at the net.

demanding lobs and increase their length as the smasher finds his rhythm. Lob-and-smash straight up and down the court, and then from the left side to the right side, and vice versa.

Start with single feeds and then go for a lob-and-smash rally, to simulate a match situation. Compete with your practice partner, the lobbing partner scoring 'one' each time the ball is smashed out or into the net. The first one to reach ten wins.

Above: A practice for accuracy with the baseline 'feeders' hitting simple balls for the volleyers who aim to hit targets on court.

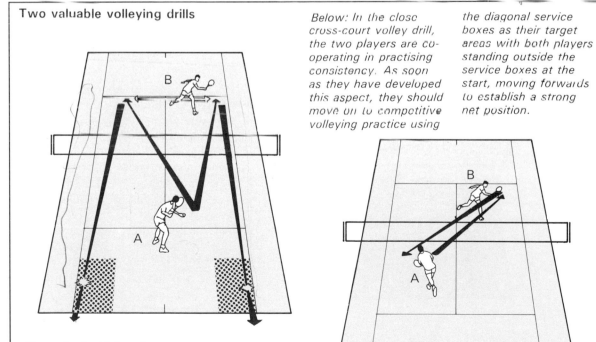

Two valuable volleying drills

Below: In the close cross-court volley drill, the two players are co-operating in practising consistency. As soon as they have developed this aspect, they should move on to competitive volleying practice using the diagonal service boxes as their target areas with both players standing outside the service boxes at the start, moving forwards to establish a strong net position.

Above: In the high volley drill, player A is helping player B to develop his technique and accuracy. He is hitting single balls to player B who aims at the shaded target areas.

Practising the service

The following routines can be practised in the same way, whether you are using a basic, topspin or slice service, or a mixture of them.

Service golf

Divide the area of each of the four service courts by a marker half-way between the centre and singles sidelines. Imagine a line running through each marker from the net to the service line. The object of the practice is to improve accuracy as well as stroke quality, which should of course be maintained or improved throughout any practice session.

If you are by yourself, start from the deuce court and serve at the outside half of the service court until you have served a ball into that area. Relating the scoring to golf, if your third service is the first one in the area, then you have 'holed' in three. Then from the same position, aim at the inside half of the same court and so get your score for the second hole. Move to the advantage court for two more holes, and then to the other end of the court for four more holes, making eight in all. Record your total score for the round of eight holes. After some practice, aiming at areas for which you had a high score, play another round to try to improve on your first total score. The game can be played in pairs, or even fours, like golf, scoring as for stroke play.

Service golf is particularly good for developing a spin service which may be fairly new to you, or for developing greater power, or for practising the start of a move towards the net.

In 'matchplay' service golf, each player in turn aims for the 'hole', while the other practises his return of service. If you score 2 and your practice partner scores 3, you have won the first hole. Complete a round of the eight holes in this way. As your accuracy improves, split each court into three areas, instead of two, and you have a round of twelve much more demanding holes!

First and second services

In a match a second service follows if the first one is a fault. It is sensible to practise serving in this rotation, so that you get used to changing the skill needed for one type of service to the skill required for a second delivery.

Play a first service, followed by a second service from the deuce court. Repeat the process from the advantage court and then move to the other end of the court to serve two more pairs of services. If you do three circuits of the court, twelve attempts are involved. Keep a record of how many first and how many second services are in, and try to improve the ratio of first to second, while working hard to eliminate double faults!

Use the above ideas to practise the service generally, but make a point of working on a specific skill or fault. It might be to gain greater control of spin, or to increase the power of your first service. Check your improvement

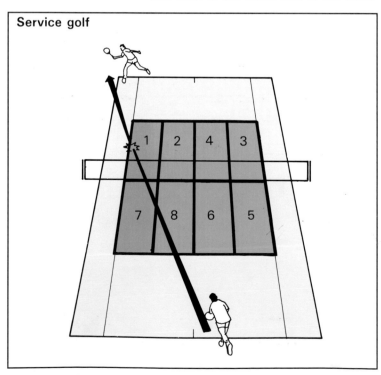

Service golf

Far left: The player practising ball placement shows an excellent release position of the left hand but a less than efficient take-back of the racket with the right hand. Practice should make perfect!

Left: A good example of the pronation of the racket hand after contact with the ball. Notice the player's concentration — both eyes on the ball

in the selected area and when it is incorporated confidently in your service, move onto another.

Practise for power

It is sometimes a good idea to work on power alone, without thinking much about accuracy. Serve flat out, without inhibition either on the court or into stop netting. This is a very good way of developing muscle strength and a smooth powerful serving action.

Another way is to practise throwing a ball as far and high as possible, using the overarm action, which is closely related to the action of 'throwing' the racket at the ball when serving. A tennis ball is fine for this exercise, but a heavier ball of similar size will call for more muscle power and fluidity.

Below: This practice is designed to encourage the server to develop depth and penetration on the serve. Server A tries to hit the ball into the back section of the service box and earn three points. The aim is to achieve a maximum 30 points from 10 serves. His secondary consideration is to develop penetration on the serve, gaining three points for a ball bouncing on the second bounce in section 3. The aim is to score a maximum 30 points from 10 serves.

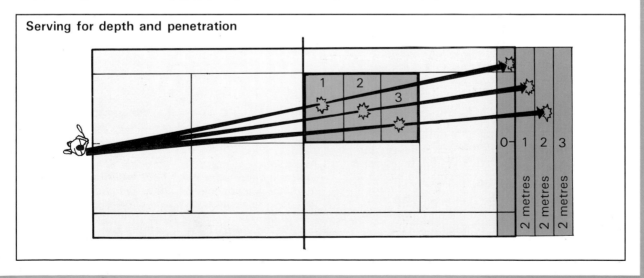

Serving for depth and penetration

Advanced drills

The main objectives of practice are to improve strokes and their use, and to develop parts of matchplay, such as tactical serving, return of service, rallying and net-play.

Advanced practice to improve strokes and their use is best carried out through drills, which should aim at technique, development, accuracy, power as required and consistency. Those for groundstrokes, volleys, the services and other tactics at a more basic level have been outlined already.

Develop basic practices to a higher standard

To develop accuracy, set yourself targets relative to your standard of play, reducing their size as your accuracy improves. To help you to work technically, at a basic level, your practice partner should 'feed' repetitively to roughly the same area. A friend, who need not himself be a tennis player,

can throw or hit single balls to you. Progress to 'pattern' feeding of various kinds, such as one short ball and then a longer length one, or to one side and then to the other.

● Progress to yet more unpredictable feeding, so that the ball comes to either side of you, and to varying lengths. In this way anticipation, and reading the flight of the ball, are practised as well as the actual strokes involved. Combine the greater challenge from unpredictable feeding with aiming for smaller target areas.

● Bring in *tactical choice* of shot to these practices, with a choice of targets, forcing early decisions as to which one you will aim for.

● Bring in the *varieties* of strokes, flat, slice and topspin, and practise rapid decision making as to which one you will use for each shot.

● In the volleying drills, use the same progression of difficulty and gradually

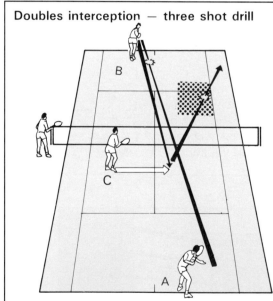

Doubles interception — three shot drill

Above: The doubles interception drill. The purpose is to give the net player the opportunity to practise his interception of the receiver's cross-court return. Player A serves to the middle of the service box. Player B returns the ball to A and player C must intercept every return and hit into the shaded area.

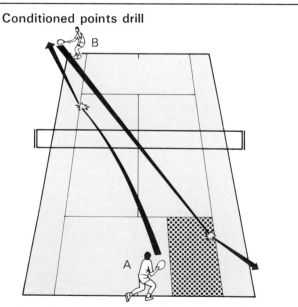

Conditioned points drill

Above: This conditioned points practice develops a common matchplay situation of serve and return of serve. The conditions are that player A must serve wide to player B's forehand who must then return the ball deep cross-court into the shaded area. After these two shots, the point is played out as normal.

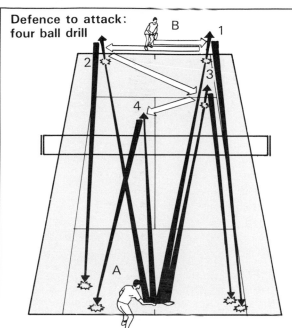

Defence to attack: four ball drill

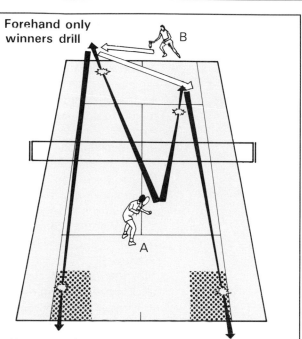

Forehand only winners drill

Above: Defence to attack (four ball) drill. The aim is to develop the transition from defence to attack, Player A feeds four single ball shots:
1 *To player B's backhand side.*
2 *To the forehand side.*

3 *To the short-length approach backhand.*
4 *To a forehand volley. He then repeats the sequence. Player B must play all shots into specified areas of the court. There are many variations on this theme.*

Above: Forehand only winners drill. The aim is to develop the forehand into a powerful attacking shot. Player A feeds single balls to player B who must play every shot on the forehand. Player A mixes deep balls with

medium-short balls down the centre. Player B must move quickly to the ball in order to set up an attacking forehand. Player B counts the number of successful shots in each series.

introduce both the drive volley and the stop volley with the drill.

● Play against yourself by having a form of scoring. This can be one point for each successful shot, or for each time you hit your chosen target.

Plan each part of a practice session

To give purpose to your practice, it is important to work out carefully the size and position of the target and the type of feeding you need. If there is more than one target, in what tactical positions are you going to place them? One example would be to have one deep target to one side of the court, a short one to the other side and a third target deep in the middle of the court for safety shots.

You should also decide which strokes you want to include, and which variations on them. Finally there is the question of the scoring system

you will use, against yourself or a practice partner. You do not need a professional coach to work out these details, although this would be very helpful. You can analyze your own game, and plan your practice sessions purposefully, one part at a time.

Practise the mental side

Practise the use of concentration and determination and other important mental qualities that help you to improve, and to be a good match player. How you practise has a direct effect on how you play in matches. Sloppy, purposeless practices lead to poor match performance. If you do not do your best in practice it is unlikely that you will produce your best in competition, but if you keep a lively attitude of mind in practice, always trying to improve and develop, you will enjoy the effort and see the results in your match performance.

Advanced practices for matchplay

Advanced practices should relate as directly as possible to competitive play so that a practice can be transferred readily to competition. Drills are excellent for improving strokes, accuracy and concentration while they, too, should be related to targets and stroke use in matchplay. Thus the pitfall of becoming a good stroke player but a poor performer in matchplay can be avoided and all-round skill developed.

Threes

Practice can be fun even at the advanced level, when you are striving in earnest towards becoming a better class of player. However, there should always be a serious purpose in mind. If you have a number of other people with whom to practise, 'threes' is a good way of simulating pressured match situations of various kinds.

With one player against two, all playing in a singles court, the player on his own is put under more pressure than he usually meets in matchplay. With each of the two players having to cover only half of a singles court, they should be able to return very consistently. So rallies are prolonged while tactical situations can be set up by the pair of players moving the single one around the court. They can play with a mixture of long and short length shots as well as hitting, alternately or at random, to either side of him.

The single player may be playing only groundstrokes, or he may prefer to concentrate on volleys and smashes by basing himself inside the service courts. He can also practise making approach shots off shorter length balls, then moving towards the net to volley from the attacking zone.

Do not use this valuable practice as a substitute for physical training, with the net player running a lot, but hitting aimlessly. He should play every shot with a sound selection of stroke, and a definite tactical purpose. Encouraged by the two players to chase every ball,

1

his fitness will be tested and improved in any case, while he is also gaining realistic match practice.

Court surfaces

The player who is getting up to a higher standard of play should take or make every opportunity to practise on a wide variety of court surfaces. Only in this way can he learn to adapt to playing matches on slow, medium-paced and fast courts, and to adjust to the various footholds and frictional 'feel' that different surfaces provide (see pages 66 and 67).

Wind and sun

The only way to get the best from yourself in windy or bright sunlight conditions is to practise in them. So do not always choose to practise with the sun behind you, but make a point of playing, and especially serving, with the sun in your eyes. In a match you have no choice in the matter: you have to take your turn at either end. Play in strong wind, too, whenever possible, and look again at pages 68 and 69 to see how, by getting used to difficult playing conditions, you can not only avoid being put off by them but can make them work to your advantage!

Left: The single player in the foreground is practising volleying under pressure. The two players at the back of the court are hitting the ball alternately to his forehand and backhand sides. This is a good practice for developing mobility and fitness.

Left: The two players in the background have hit an attacking volley followed by a short-length volley, which forces the player in the foreground to move backwards to the deep ball and forwards to the shorter ball. This practice is good for encouraging the single player to move quickly from defence into attack.

Practise parts of matchplay

Look again at the tactical situations described in Chapter 4. Select an area that is a high priority for you to improve. It might be serve-and-volleying, or using spin as a tactic, or playing the early ball, or using the wind to your best advantage. Over a period of time, select other parts of the game to work on specifically, perhaps the return of service, or using the lob tactically. So build up your game and at the same time experience the enjoyment that comes with your growing tennis strengths and skills.

Serve-and-volley practice

Constantly check your level of efficiency in the various aspects and subdivisions of the game, and practise to develop your strengths and eliminate your weaknesses. For instance, if you have chosen serve-and-volleying you may have decided that serving is your strongest area, and the movement between your serving and playing the first volley is the weakest. You may have decided, too, that the movement problem affects the efficiency of your

volleys, particularly against low balls on the forehand side. In this case you could choose three practices.

To develop your serving strength further concentrate on either accuracy, consistency or pace, but also check that you are moving off towards the net quickly after you have served. Perhaps an adjustment to the way you bring in your back leg as you take the first step forwards would get you off the mark more quickly. Practise the service and the take-off after it, in a realistic situation with a practice partner returning your service, so that you can complete the serve-and-volley procedure.

For quicker movement, pick up speed quickly for three or four long fast strides towards the net. To improve balance, check just after crossing the service line, gathering yourself to move to intercept the receiver's return, or to move back to smash if you are lobbed. Check your low forehand volley in a drill situation, making any technical adjustments that you feel are necessary. Then include

Low volley practice

Right: The aim of the low volley practice is to develop a player's ability to play low volleys to a consistent length. Player A stands in mid-court and does not move forward to the net, but stays in 'no man's land'. Player B aims to hit the ball into the target area.

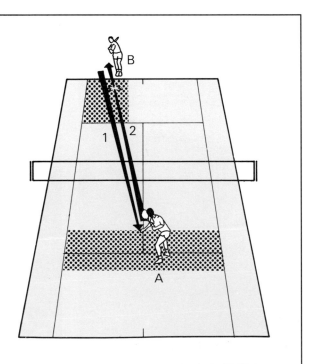

the low volley in the practice points by getting your practice partner to return the ball in such a way that you can play that stroke. (If he finds this is too difficult to do consistently, then he can hit a ball from his hand, just as your service ball is passing by him, to provide the shot that you want.) Play the point out after the low volley so that you practise recovery from it ready for your next shot. Remember that no shot can be perfected in isolation – you must be ready to move into it from a preceding stroke and move on to play the next.

Choose other practices

With the detailed plan above as an example, create suitable practice situations for other parts of matchplay. Concentrate on one selected area of the whole skill (returning the service,

for example) or a whole sequence, such as a groundstroke approach followed by a volley. After you have improved one area, turn to another. By doing this you are building up a part of the game that is very important in matchplay, and then transferring it to competition will be easier after you have played plenty of practice points in which you have concentrated particularly on that tactic.

Use targets

As for all practices, introduce targets where applicable, and a form of scoring against yourself or against a practice partner. A form of scoring against yourself sets goals for improvement in subsequent practices, while the use of targets and scoring is invariably a greater aid to interest and therefore to concentration.

Serve-and-volley stabilizing practices

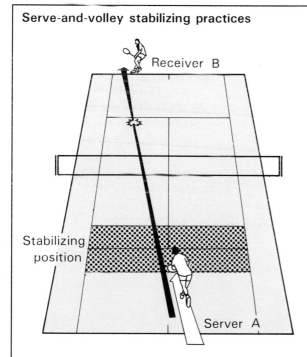

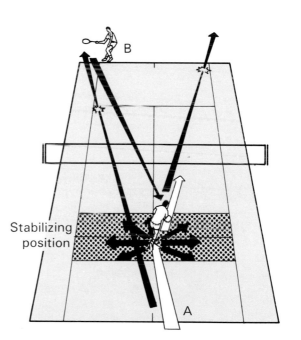

Above: This practice is to develop the server's ability to reach a good volleying position as far forward as possible before the opponent strikes the ball. The server moves quickly forward after serving and has to stop just as his opponent is about to strike the ball. He should then mark the position he has reached on court and subsequently try to improve on that position in practice.

Above: In this practice the server should stabilize for the first volley in mid-court and then continue forward to adopt a strong attacking net position. Player B feeds one gentle return to A's first volley. Player A plays his shot deep to the backhand and moves into the net. Player B then tries to win the point with a lob or passing shot.

Relate your strategy to your practice

Planning for a practice session is fun, while the session will prove to be far more valuable if you are aiming at definite goals, instead of practising casually or at random.

If you wish to work on the technique of a stroke choose first from the main strokes, which are the service, forehand, backhand, high volleys, low volleys, smash and lob. There are, of course, variations around all these strokes, so it may be a variation that you choose to practise; perhaps developing an attacking lifted backhand to add to a sound sliced one?

Alternatively, you may wish to improve the technique of one of the lesser used shots, which are the drop shot, half volley and recovery shot. The drive volley and stop volley are actually variations of the volley, but are sometimes treated as separate strokes.

Work on a part of your game
Think through the areas of the game, roughly in the order in which they may be played. How do you perform in each of the areas? If you are physically fit and quite strong, could that strength be developed further through practice? If you assess yourself as weak in an area then work on it in a practice session, but work sensibly on a mixture of your strengths and weaknesses. Do not fall into the trap of working only on weaknesses as this can develop into a negative approach to practising.

These areas cover the situations which you create or meet during a match. When you have chosen from them for the matchplay part of your practice session, turn to the sections on game plans and tactics (Chapters 2, 3 and 4) for advice on each of them.

The objectives of practice
The final objective of practice is that you improve as a tennis player, who can construct points well. Points add up to games, games to sets, and sets to matches. Good performance, relative to your standard of play, is based on the quality of a long series of points.

It is sometimes valuable to practise strokes which are separated from matchplay or point situations, so that the mind can be directed towards improving technique without the pressures that stem from competition. It is equally important to train physically through exercises outside the game, such as running, weight training, circuit training, stretching and the like, but it is more important to relate practice and training as near as possible to the requirements of the game.

Thus physical training should often include the movements which are required for playing tennis, such as side-stepping, swerving, moving backwards on balance, getting off the mark quickly, jumping for a smash, bending from the knees to play a low ball and sprinting on balance.

Check through your physical assets and liabilities and practise to improve them, often with a racket in your hand while playing imaginary strokes. Then you are training with greater realism in relation to tennis, and your improving fitness will be transferred more readily to the matchplay situation.

Practise stroke play
Similarly with your strokes, practise them in areas of the game such as the return of service, or playing passing shots. Work for improvement in technique but also towards the understanding, and feel, of the adjustments needed to use the strokes well in a variety of tennis situations.

In general, you need to adjust your stroke when playing to attack from the one you use to play a defensive shot. How you play the ball when it is rushing you is different from how you treat it when you have plenty of time to play your stroke. For the latter you need an earlier and shorter take-back of the racket, and perhaps an improved body

position as an alternative to a full swing from your favoured hitting position, when you have more time to prepare for and play the stroke.

Select your practices

You should therefore select one of the main areas of playing tennis in which to practise your use of strokes:

● Serving.
● Returning the service.
● Rallying with the hope of being able to attack, but aware of the need to defend at times.
● Moving towards the net to volley.
● Being in the net area ready to volley, or smash and to intercept in doubles.
● Playing passing shots.
● Using the lob.
● Using the drop shot.
● Using the stop volley.

In serving, you need to practise more than an improving service action. Practise aiming so that you can serve tactically in relation to your opponent. Practise changing from one type of service to another: for example, from the attempt at an ace with the first service, to a deep spin service. Practise serving with a practice partner returning, so that you learn to recover quickly ready for the next shot.

Practise the body movement required to get off the mark quickly to serve-and-volley. Thus you will not only be improving your technique, power and accuracy and consistency but you will be improving your ability as a server — not just having a good service in isolation, but being unable to use it well in matchplay.

Try similar procedures with all the other areas of the game so that your improving *strokes* are constantly improving in their *context*, that is to say in the various situations which occur during points.

Practices in isolation are valuable for short periods but can become boring and rather pointless unless you are particularly dedicated. Have fun and gain satisfaction by working for improvement in selected areas of your game, and then see how much you have improved in point construction, and therefore as a match player!

Above: Baseline defence versus net attack with the players in the foreground hitting lobs for the net players to smash. In this practice, if the defending players can hit the ball past the smashers they should then take over the attacking net position, and the other pair revert to baseline defence.

Chapter 7 **Match Preparation**

The extent of the preparation for a match will be affected by its importance to the player, and the time he has available beforehand. It is of little use to suggest to a player who is rushing from his office to get to his club in time that he prepares methodically. His main concern would be to get to the club in time to change before going onto the court.

For a casual, recreational match a brief unstructured warm up session may be thought sufficient, but to gain the maximum enjoyment from the game it is really important to take a more considered view of match preparation. At the end of the scale, to rush into a match without adequate mental and physical preparation reduces your chances of playing your best, at the other it can actually be harmful. No strenuous exercise should be taken either immediately after food or on an empty stomach.

Here are some suggestions for getting the most out of a tennis match, whether played as a 'friendly' or in serious competition. Try to fit in a pre-match practice earlier in the day of the match. Ensure that your muscles are relaxed, and practise the strokes and tactics to be used later on.

Have a light meal not less than an hour before the match is due to start. Leave the celebrations until the evening, after you have won the match!

Be ready

Check your kit and equipment, making sure that you have with you everything you will need and that the strings of your racket(s) are sound.

Just before going on to court, carry out a short varied series of bending, stretching and suppleness exercises to help loosen up your muscles.

Make the best use possible of the warm up rallies and practice serves before the match. Make this a structured period with clear objectives (see pages 106 and 107).

After the match

Have an inquest on your preparation as well as on your performance in the match itself. A check on the effectiveness of your preparation for one match may yield valuable lessons to remember on future occasions.

Take some notes on your opponent's strengths and weaknesses and on the principal points of the match. It is useful to have these details in a diary for future reference, whether or not you expect to meet that particular opponent again. If you do, it will be a help in preparing your tactics to exploit his weaknesses and combat his strengths, but any record of how your tactics have worked against a particular type of player will be an aid to future planning.

Above. Ivan Lendl has shown the benefits of disciplined preparation in his outstanding record of consistency in matchplay. His early years of training in Czechoslovakia sowed the seeds for his phenomenal success.

Opposite: John Lloyd and Chris Evert walk off-court after a practice session. All players should prepare thoroughly in order to be at their most effective in matchplay.

The vital five minutes

The warm up time

At the beginning of every tennis match played under International Tennis Federation rules five minutes are allowed on court before play commences. If you watch the top players, you will see that they usually use this time to send down a highly impressive series of powerful serves, no doubt intended as much to impress their opponent and the watching public as to perfect any technical point. However, they will usually also practise a selection of drives and other specimen strokes, and the opposing players, especially in a doubles match, may rally the ball until the umpire calls for play to commence.

During the warm up, the players will probably keep on a sweater or a track suit top even if the weather is warm. This is to speed up the process by which the muscles regain their flexibility after a period of inaction.

If you watch casual or recreational tennis players, however, or a tournament, you will often notice that there is very little pattern to the way in which they use this period. Some players will send the ball back and forth across the net, usually at random, for considerably longer than five minutes before deciding to get on with their game or match. Others simply try to copy the famous players and set out to impress everybody who is watching by delivering a series of tremendous serves and blistering smashes.

Use the warm up sensibly

In fact, the warm up time before play can have a very important part in improving your tennis performance: you should always use the vital five minutes to advance important areas of play dealt with elsewhere in this book.

● Improve your technique. There may be strokes you want to check; look for opportunities to use these strokes, not going aggressively for outright winners when rallying with your opponent, but keeping the ball in play and concentrating on accuracy.

● Mental awareness. The warm up is the only chance you will have to start thinking tennis. Before going onto the court your mind has been occupied with other things, and now it must be brought exclusively to bear on the game. Use the time to start developing your game plans.

● Analyze your game. Decide what your strengths and weaknesses are on this particular day, and use the time to check the strokes that are working well for you and those that are giving you some trouble.

● Assess your opponent. If you have played him before, build on the picture you have already formed of his game. If you have never played against one another, now is your chance to find out whether he is fast on his feet, better on his backhand or the forehand, good at anticipating, aggressive or steady by nature. Remember that once you have started to play the first point it will be too late. The warm up is the only chance you will have to prepare for the match.

Physical preparation

You may have taken heed of the advice given on page 104 concerning preparation for the match, but however fit you may be the demands on your body during what may turn out to be a long period of strenuous exertion are very much greater than they were before.

Keep on a sweater, with long sleeves, at least for the first part of the warm up. If the air is cold, the warm-up will be needed literally, but even on a hot day the muscles need to adjust from the inactive to the active state.

The muscles require oxygen, and this is brought to them by the blood. When you are sitting, or moving slowly, the smaller blood vessels in the arms and legs contract. By warming up

Left: Jeremy Bates (Great Britain) warms up prior to matchplay. At this stage, he will be trying to groove his method and develop a rhythm whilst adapting to the speed of the court and his opponent's shots. He will also evaluate his opponent's strengths and weaknesses.

gradually, releasing tensions, stretching stiff limbs without straining them, the circulation is given time to cope with the heavy demands for oxygen supply that come with active play. It can be actually harmful to put sudden strain on muscles that are not prepared for it. Be positive. Use the warm up constructively and with purpose and it could make an important contribution to your success.

The rules for warming up
Five minutes are allowed for warming up before a match or after a break of more than twenty minutes. Three minutes are allowed after a break in play of between six and twenty minutes.

Practice matches

These are ideal for introducing new facets to your game. Play your normal game during practice matches while adding one area for improvement from each of a few selected areas. For instance, you may decide to introduce a stroke that is new to you, and practise it as often as possible during the practice match to build up your skill and confidence so that eventually it can be added to your stroke repertoire during actual matchplay.

Additionally, you can select a specific tactic and play it not only to improve your skill, but also to discover what counters your practice opponent uses against it. Most importantly of all, you will learn to use the new stroke to your best advantage. You should also work on a particular aspect of your mental approach to matchplay. For example, you might choose to develop your ability to concentrate, then assess your performance in retrospect, to see if you were successful and were able to concentrate with greater intensity, and for longer periods.

Below: No matter how much you practise, there is always the unexpected! You do not expect in a doubles match to find your partner on the other side of the net! In this match at Wimbledon, Bob Lutz in the foreround, has fallen over the net into the opponents' court in an attempt to pick up a drop shot, while his partner collapses in mock despair. Three versus one is not fair!

Develop your strategy

In order to do this, you might choose to play with greater aggression than usual. In this way, you can use the practice match to discover *when* it is best to attack and what types of balls are most vulnerable to your attack. Alternatively, you may be playing too aggressively and need to develop more patience. If this is the case for you, try to be less impetuous and more patient in the practice match, so that when you attack, it is against a suitable ball in a profitable position.

Is there a need to improve your matchplay behaviour?

You can use practice matches to improve your behaviour on court and cut out tantrums, swearing or other emotional outbursts. You can also concentrate on being more positive and less inclined to complain if you lose a point or become despondent. If you concentrate on behaving with greater self-control in practice matches then you can do this also in

real matchplay, and thus play more positively and successfully.

Plan for each practice match

Select one aspect from each of the following – strokes, tactics, fitness and your mental approach. Then try to include all your choices in a practice match. Analyze your performance and attitude after the match to see if you have progressed. By doing this, you can transfer any improvements in your practice game into your matchplay and thereby widen, and improve, your overall game.

Orthodox sets, or three set matches, are invaluable. It is worthwhile to consider the following alternatives for a practice session – to create interest and change; to make the best possible use of limited time available; or to adapt the practice to a specific situation. The purpose of these structures should be obvious.

● Play a match of tie-breaks instead of sets – perhaps the best of three or five or seven tie-breaks.

● Play a five-set match with the starting score in each set four games-all.

● Play a two-set match, which could be a draw, with the starting score 4-1 up in one set and 1-4 down in the next, or vice versa.

● Use table tennis scoring, serving five points each in turn, and play to be the first to 11, 15 or 21 points.

● Play without volleys, smashes or drop-shots, with either player losing the point if his ball lands in either of the service courts.

● Make a rule that you must serve-and-volley on every point.

● The stronger of two practice opponents has only one service, whereas the weaker player starts at 15-0 up on his service.

● Both players have only one service.

A final word of advice: to get the most out of these practice match sessions always play at the same intensity as you would in an actual match situation.

Above: Peter Lundgren and Jeremy Bates in consultation during a match. The most successful doubles pairs communicate well during matches in order to adapt and develop tactics and strategy during the match.

Chapter 8 **The Mental Game**

The importance of good attitudes

The importance of the mental role in top level sport has long been realized. Nowadays there are a number of sports psychologists whose work is to help individuals or teams to achieve their best physical performance.

The entourage of tutor, coach, physiotherapist and others, which accompanies some top players during their travels would be incomplete without a psychologist who specializes in inducing positive attitudes to competition. Hypnosis has even been used to help to remove those inhibitions which prevent a player or a team from producing their best form.

For a club or recreational player such intensive attention to the mental side of tennis might be considered as being out of proportion. To come to a club tournament with a psychologist and a hypnotist to prepare a player for the Mixed Doubles final would be rather excessive! Yet thinking in a way which enhances performance, at any level, is surely acceptable and sensible.

The mental approach to matchplay is the driving force behind performance. If the mind is thinking badly the player is handicapped, with his capabilities in strokes and tactics constantly eluding him.

Good gamesmanship

'The spirit of the game' is not an old fashioned concept, but admirable in any age. The so-called 'professional foul' in football is no more than an euphemism for cheating, and the offender should be sent off in disgrace immediately. So it is with tennis, in which the deliberate putting off of an opponent is as unacceptable as the deliberate foul in other sports.

To want to play well, fervently hoping for a win, but strong enough mentally not to complain if you lose is the right mental approach to a tennis match at any level of play.

Start with confidence and maintain it by resolving that nothing is going to disturb you from trying your best with every shot, like Michael Chang who provides an excellent example of concentration. Clear your mind from one point before starting the next, so that there is no chance of a poorly played point remaining in your mind to sap your confidence. Remove your fear of losing by the procedure of playing *one point at a time*. Your mind will have no room for the alarming thought that you might lose. Thinking ahead to winning is equally dangerous though, as a player can get over-confident and then try to finish the match off with a series of great winners, which is usually a disastrous policy! Alternatively, he can become over-cautious through fear of losing from a winning position, and just play the ball back, while hoping that the opponent will make enough mistakes to lose. The opponent will gain confidence from the removal of pressure, and is likely to climb back into the match. Think right, and keep on with the type of game which took you to a leading position, and play it well, point after point.

Check your behaviour

Accept utterly and finally that tantrums, excuses and complaining are the signs of weakness, and that the strong minded have no time for them. Remember that the strength of his desire to win cannot be measured by the amount of fuss or number of excuses made by a player when he is losing or has lost. All competitors want very much to win, but some have enough mental strength to behave graciously when they have lost, while others, including a very few at world class level, cannot stand the pressure of disappointment!

Luck plays a part in all games, except perhaps chess which is often considered to be the purest contest of all. Perhaps luck in tennis has to be deserved, or is only available to optimists? So believe in it, and good fortune may favour you at times when you feel in need of a stroke of luck. However it is more likely that you will benefit more by acting than just hoping, so consider Gary Player's remark while he was practising his putting in the dusk after a long and tiring day of matchplay: 'The more I practise, the luckier I get!'.

Stroke play and mental quality

Strokes and their use in *tactics, fitness,* and *mental approaches* are the four main ingredients of tennis performance. Strokes can be evaluated for consistency, power and accuracy. Onlookers can see, and opponents feel the effect of good or poor tactical play. Fitness, however, can be measured factually and accurately.

There is sometimes a tendency to rate players and select them for teams on the quality of their strokes, the soundness and wiliness of their tactics, and the degree of their fitness. Yet the invisible driving forces behind the visible aspects of playing should be rated as highly, and perhaps the highest of all. Unseen they may be, but their importance is paramount.

Two types of mental quality

One is the *thinking* side, which decides on strategy and tactics and when to change them, while it remains aware of how a match is progressing. The thinking side is of vital importance too, to get the most from practice through an ability to understand and learn, and to self-analyze for strengths and weaknesses.

The other side of the mind is the *emotional* one, from which stems the courage, determination, concentration, competitiveness and that vital but elusive mental trait, confidence, that are among other valuable attitudes of mind.

● Concentration governs consistency through preparing well, and producing one's best, stroke after stroke.
● Confidence prevents inhibitions from taking over to reduce valuable aggression to timidity in playing.
● Competitiveness is an emotional mental attitude from which springs the determination to do one's best, to find a way to win, and to relish being part of a tough match.
● 'Think high and walk tall' is a desirable positive attitude. It takes courage to keep on thinking positively if you are well behind in the score and playing below form, but it can be achieved.

Many attitudes lie dormant

These are partly hereditary and partly fostered through environment. Too many people think that only others have the type of attitudes that lead to success. But at all standards of play, good positive attitudes add to the enjoyment and satisfaction which can be gained from competitive tennis. So look for them, find them, and nurse them to greater strength.

Training the mind

Every muscular action you take is first decided on by your brain, either after thought, or instinctively. So the 'order' to play a stroke, where to aim, or when to move comes from the mind, and it is the mind which must be trained first. The muscle and the brain work together as a unit, and in training should be treated as a partnership.

The thought processes are given more time at change of ends than during the playing of a point. Between points there is enough time to plan for the point to come, but some players make the excuse that once play has started, there is no time to think. Fortunately we can, with experience, make many tennis playing decisions on the instinctual level, a vital ability in fast matchplay, or when receiving a service from a powerful opponent. In these situations, with only a fraction of a second to play the ball, there really is no time for conscious thought. Anticipation, and even sometimes guesswork, as to which side the ball will arrive, and an instinctive response to reach and return the ball are necessary when faced with fast pace services.

Instinct or decision?
Reasoned reaction, deliberation and decision making are linked, as are instinctive reaction, reflex and habit.

Right: Ivan Lendl in his habitual stance prior to serving. He goes through a ritual of movements in preparing to serve, which frees his mind from any doubts and focuses his attention purely on positive goals.

Experience at making decisions speeds the thought process, until thought-out reactions become instinctive ones. One example might be when a wide gap in your opponent's court is offered to you. Here there is no need for consideration. An experienced player hits instinctively at the gap because he has done so many times before, and has proved it to be a good policy in the past.

Similarly, the experienced player will know when to attack and when to defend and, for example, when to play a lob volley or a drop-shot. Previous experience leads him to the right conclusions, so he can react instinctively or by habit. The court situation before him, his knowledge of the opposing player's game, his assessment of the conditions, the dictates of the game plan he is following and, of course, the pressure he is under all combine in the experienced player's choice of shot in a given set of circumstances.

However, not all decisions should be allowed to become instinctive. Your specific target, the type of service to be used, and whether or not you are going to move into the net behind it, are three considered decisions that should be made before your service every time. While preparing to smash there is just enough time to decide on your aim. The same applies in a rally of deep balls on a slow surface, and when preparing to return a reduced pace second service. Even so, time is very limited, and a match player needs an alert mind, very aware of the situation during a point so that he can react quickly to his opponent's tactics.

Practice to develop instinct
The only way to develop a soundly thought-out tactic or decision to the point where it becomes second nature, is through constant practice. For this purpose, practising in match situations is best. Repetitious practice of a stroke or tactic will refine your technique, but

Left: Ilie Nastase in a relaxed position at the change-over. Most players use this time to plan their tactics and strategy, and dispel any negative thinking prior to stepping back onto the court and commencing battle.

making mastery of that stroke or technique instinctive requires it to be presented regularly but unexpectedly. If you practise with the aim of developing quick thinking and quick judgement you will soon see your reactions developing into reflexes.

Reflexes or reactions?

The best, and perhaps only, way to speed reflexes, which can be defined as actions which take place without any conscious thought at all, is to practise in situations in which a quick reflex is needed because there is no time for thought.

● Volley in pairs, with the players close together and hitting the ball hard.

● Try to volley from near the service line against a smash off a short lob.

● Defend with groundstrokes, including half-volleys, from just inside the baseline against volleys hit down hard from the net by feeders.

The mind needs training for tennis just as much as the body does. This can be a very enjoyable process. You will feel great satisfaction when you find that you are getting back balls which formerly would have seemed impossible to return. With quicker decision making, and more good habits being formed so that your instinctive play improves, you will find that you gain time to out-think your opponent more often.

Temperament

To get the best from tennis at all levels it should never be forgotten that it is a competitive game. It follows that a player should care whether he wins or loses, and do all he can, within the written and unwritten rules of the game, to try to beat his opponent. It is easy to appear to be a good loser if you do not mind losing! It is not always easy to accept defeat with a good grace when you have been extending every nerve and sinew to win. It is even more difficult if your opponent has shown signs of ruthlessness or unsportsmanlike playing. However, the rewards of the game to both players, as well as to anyone who may be watching, are vastly increased if both winner and loser face the result, whatever it may be, with dignity.

Bad behaviour

Petulant behaviour and the making of excuses are often regretted later, once the offender has cooled down and put his disappointment in a better perspective. To lose well is often misunderstood as being a sign that the loser did not have enough will to win – enough of the killer instinct. This is usually not the case. The tough-minded competitor tries his hardest to win, but is strong enough mentally to

Above right: Steffi Graf is deep in thought, possibly focusing her attention on the point ahead. She shows excellent temperament and behaviour at all times, no matter how difficult the situation.

Below: John McEnroe shows some of the emotion and frustration that have been synonymous with his playing career. Although he appears 'down' in this picture, he is renowned for bouncing back and even playing better when he is emotionally stimulated.

accept defeat gracefully. Resisting temptation is a sign of a tough, resilient mind. In fact, the player who controls his natural disappointment after losing, resolving to benefit from the lessons he has learned, is more likely to win the next match he plays.

There will always be characters who cannot properly accept that they might have lost because the other player was better on the day. Through self-pity they turn to excuses, or through ill manners they behave unpleasantly during the match, and after it if they have lost. Their tennis progress is severely handicapped. To blame bad luck, bad conditions or bad umpiring decisions for a defeat is to hide from the truth. It could be argued that no one ever lost a match entirely for these

reasons. A defeat should always be regarded as an opportunity for self analysis and for improvement.

Don't make excuses

Try as hard as you can, never give up, get sorry for yourself, or make excuses. Once a player has what he thinks of as a good excuse in his mind his resolve weakens. 'How can I possibly do well with this badly sprained ankle?' he may say after he has slightly twisted the joint. 'Now I don't have to try, as everyone will see why I lost!'

Accept that nearly all matches are won because the winner has played better than the loser. Genuine injury affects the result of a tiny minority of matches. But how can one player argue that he lost because of the wind, sun, court surface, or any other condition which is exactly the same for both players? If you can accept different conditions, indifferent umpiring, lucky shots against you, or vastly superior opposition, you will be a strong competitor, a good person to have in a team and a player who is respected by everyone.

Win with modesty; be generous to the loser. After all, you know now how you would feel in his place. Avoid patronizing him during and after a match, and avoid tactless remarks like 'I felt I played very badly' to someone you have just beaten. To win with grace is another test of strength of character. It is important to analyze

your game, even when you win, and see where you could have played even better. And be ready to admit it if luck and circumstances were on your side on that occasion.

Examine your behaviour

A player who sets, and keeps to, very high standards of sporting behaviour has a clear conscience. Then his concentration can be turned entirely to the strategy and tactics during a match and his performance will be better. The game of tennis has plenty of examples of sportsmanlike behaviour in both defeat and victory. In her long and distinguished career Chris Evert has been a model of generous behaviour on the court, and among the top men players, Ivan Lendl very rarely allows the strain to get the better of him, although he is known as a profoundly self-critical player.

Tantrums on the court, racket throwing and swearing have unfortunately become more common than they were. Such behaviour may make the headlines, but it is always bad for the game of tennis and for the player who is involved.

Above left: Ivan Lendl, who is a great sportsman and highly professional in his attitude on court, is obviously disputing a call. However, if a situation goes against him, he has the flexibility of temperament not to allow it to affect his performance.

Above: Mats Wilander and Pat Cash, two of the world's top players, shake hands after a match. The sporting side of tennis is shown here where even in victory and defeat players can respect each other for their performance and ability.

Adopt a positive approach to winning and losing

Keeping in front

If you are ahead in a match the best advice is to continue with the game plan and tactics which have brought you into the lead. One extreme to avoid is to become much more aggressive, in an attempt to finish the match off quickly. The other is to become negative, in the hope that if you return the ball consistently then the opponent will make enough unforced errors for you to turn your lead into a win. In the first instance you may well overplay your hand through impatience. Instead of waiting for the right balls to attack, you may start to attack impetuously and make a lot of errors. This will not only let your opponent back into the match, but encourage him, while you could become frustrated and lose concentration as he begins to level the score. In the second instance your opponent will have easier balls to deal with, so he is less likely to make errors, while you will be offering him winning opportunities. In either case, the resulting easing-off of pressure, designed or through error, will encourage him by making him feel that he is playing better, as well as levelling off the score.

Therefore neither accelerate nor brake, but continue with your successful tactics, playing each point as it comes.

Fighting back from behind

Remember that no match is lost until it has been won. Fight back, point by point, with calmness, determination and, above all, hope.

If hope is lost, all is lost, and in a tennis match there should always be the expectation of eventual success, until the final point has been lost. As Pancho Gonzales, one of the greatest of all match players, once said, 'I never have doubts about the final result. If the match is a long one, I merely think that my opponent is being obstinate!'

'Play one point at a time' is the key to some almost incredible wins from behind. Jimmy Connors, another player who never gives up, was two sets and 1-4 down to Pernfors in one match, and 1-5 down to Miloslav Mecir in the final set of another, but won both matches. The form of scoring gives a player a breathing space during his climb back, as from 0-6, 0-6, 0-5 in a three-set match the opponent is still four points away from winning the match. Thus you do not have to play a series of match points against you, as can happen in table tennis. From 12-20 down in table tennis the prospect of eight match points has to be faced, which must inhibit the aggression of even the bravest player!

In tennis the early points in each game provide the opportunity for controlled aggression, as well as to change the strategy and tactics.

Change a losing game

While never giving up, or showing your opponent even momentarily that you have nearly had enough and are willing to accept defeat, try some changes to a game plan which has been unsuccessful on this occasion.

In overall strategy you may decide to take a few more chances if you feel that you have played too negatively.

Below: John McEnroe (not measuring the net!) appears to carry the weight of the world on his shoulders at this moment in his match.

Left: Michael Chang shows the elation of winning but during his matches he handles the shifting fortunes of matchplay with a calm and pragmatic approach.

Alternatively you may decide to be more patient before attacking, so cutting down unforced errors, if you think you have been taking too many risks.

In tactics, too, try something different. Why not switch to attacking the other side of the court, or serving more slice and less topspin, or using the lob frequently instead of trying to pass the net player with drives?

A change of direction brings new hope as well as being an excellent way of disturbing the winning pattern of your opponent. Even at the top it is remarkable how a really determined player, well down in the match, can alter the situation by winning a few key points. On such occasions the change in the attitudes of both players can be clearly seen as the player who was losing scents the possibility of victory and the other, who thought he was safe, realizes that he is still in danger. Remember that the battle is never lost or won until the last point is played. Often the greater battle is first fought in the mind. Be positive in your attitude. If you have played to your level of performance that can be classed as a win in itself.

Chapter 9 **Fit for the Game?**

General fitness

Playing tennis is an enjoyable way of contributing to normal fitness, as are stretching, walking, gardening, jogging, aerobics and playing other sports. The body needs exercise to keep it in shape and the result of neglecting exercise generally, while working sedentarily, eating and drinking too much, watching too much television, and using a car invariably instead of walking, affects adults of all ages. Children, too, can become very unfit if their lifestyle does not include enough exercise.

Exercise for normal fitness should be taken in relation to age and general physical condition. Taken daily, the mental as well as the physical benefits soon become apparent. If tennis is your main recreation, three or more sessions every week are one of many enjoyable and mentally relaxing ways of maintaining fitness. To this should be added fifteen minutes of stretching every morning, and ten minutes at night, with light exercises if a game is cancelled, to keep the muscles in tone.

Fitness for tennis

Increased general fitness is beneficial for a tennis player's performance at all levels of play. He needs to train for five main areas of fitness:
- Speed.
- Strength.
- Agility.
- Stamina.
- Suppleness.

The amount of training should be relative to your tennis goals. The player who is ambitious to be an international player must undertake fitness programmes well beyond those which can be fitted into a normal working and social life. Pages 122 and 127 give some idea of the type of exercises which are necessary for those who want to attain and maintain a very high level of fitness.

For the average club player a less rigorous programme will usually be sufficient. An hour a day spent on improving body condition, as well as playing tennis and other sports, is probably the best investment of time that you can make towards physical fitness and general good health.

Select your training

The choice of exercise is wide and should be related towards the aspects of fitness which you feel need most attention, and the type of exercises that you enjoy. Skipping may bore you, but an exercise bicycle could prove to be fun and challenging.

Jogging, aerobics to music, supervised weight training once or twice a week, or physical exercises such as double knee jumps or press-ups are a few of the wide variety of methods you can choose from, according to your own personal preference.

Make time for fitness

Any exercise chosen from the above, and many others, can be fitted in to a normal working, college or school life, and there are no good reasons for not including planned exercise and sport in your lifestyle. Use variety, set yourself goals, and revel in how well you feel as a result!

Fitness fanatics lead a lifestyle which suits few people, but it suits them and they gain great benefit from their efforts. For most people sensible and regular exercise dispenses with the need to diet.

Plan your fitness programme with the aid of the ideas in the following pages, resolve to start it immediately, maintain it with variety, and you will find your general physical condition improves hand-in-hand with your tennis playing ability. As your tennis standard improves, the demands on your body will increase, so the training schedules on which you have been working may need to be revised.

Opposite: Ivan Lendl receives treatment at the change-over during a match as permitted in the rules of tennis. The world's top players often have to play with niggling aches and pains which they normally hope to overcome through treatment and sound training programmes.

General training

Some suggestions for exercise

From the suggestions that follow select the types of fitness training which appeal to you. There are numerous excellent books on training, so a visit to a library or a bookshop to supplement your own selection of sports books will help you to make the best choices.

Always warm up

Before any type of exercise or playing any kind of sport you should always warm up and stretch. By doing so you prepare your muscles for exercise, avoid the injuries which can be caused by performing violent actions with cold and taut muscles, and gain concentration ready for the enjoyment of the game to follow.

Make up simple daily fitness programmes, and vary these from week to week or month to month. Keep to the exercises which you enjoy most, but include some which bring specific benefit to a part of your body which you want to develop particularly. For example, press-ups for shoulder strength, or sit-ups to develop your abdominal muscles.

Informal training

In addition to your daily programme, there are a number of things you can do at odd times during the day. Use these and look for other opportunities for informal training.

Right: Squeezing a soft tennis ball can help develop wrist strength.

● Squeeze a squash ball, or a soft old tennis ball, one minute on, one minute off, for ten minutes. This will help your grips and strengthen your wrists.

● Step briskly upstairs, two at a time, on tiptoe. This develops feet, calves and, if prolonged, heart and lungs.

● Push hard against a wall, with one or both hands on the wall and the feet about a yard away from it.

● Sit on a chair or on the floor, grasp your leg just below the knee with fingers interlocked, and then pull with your arms while you push with your leg. Do this with each leg in turn to strengthen arms and legs.

● Breathe very deeply by an open window or out of doors. Hold your breath (for increasing amounts of time) before expelling it powerfuly through partially closed lips.

● Interlock your fingers and pull hard as if to pull them apart. This is an excellent exercise for increasing the power of your backhand.

● Tie one end of a yard-long piece of strong cord to a petrol can partly filled with water. Secure the other end of the cord to a piece of broom handle. Wind up the weight, using both hands, until it touches the broom handle, and then let it down very slowly with an unwinding motion. Repeat, and add water as you get stronger. This will improve your grip and strengthen your wrists and forearms.

These are simple but effective exercises, which require hardly any preparation or equipment, and they can be performed whenever you have a spare moment during the day. Using exercises like these is very much to be recommended as they supplement the more formal training you undertake and have the added benefit of spreading it through the day. As well as strengthening the particular muscles you need to develop your tennis technique, they will help to improve your stamina, so important for the sustained effort used in a tennis match.

Tennis training

General fitness is the basis for specific fitness for a particular sport. With good general fitness you can enjoy many types of sport, but if tennis is your favourite game, then exercises to improve the movements required for it should be used as well as other types of general training.

A tennis court circuit

Create your own tennis court circuits so that you get a variety of the movements required for playing. You may wish to make variations on the following suggestions:

● Start behind the tramlines, and sprint to the net.
● Sidestep across to the other tramline.
● Move backwards to the baseline.
● Sidestep across, back to your starting point. Thus you have moved in four directions. Time your circuit, and try to improve your times for each circuit you devise. For shorter distances, use the service and centre lines as markers for your circuit.

Interval running

Jog, sprint, jog, sprint over distances of about the width of a singles court. Change from sprinting forward to turning sideways or moving backwards so that your turn includes movements in four directions, as in tennis. Include jumping as for a smash, or to reach to play a high volley, and dipping to touch the ground. This is a similar movement to that of bending to play a low volley.

Changing direction

Put down three markers, A, B and C, about six yards apart in a triangle. Sprint, with a racket in your hand, from A to B; turn sharply, on balance, to side-step to C; turn and move backwards to A. Repeat a number of times, and increase these repetitions as greater fitness is achieved.

All exercise is of value

Planned exercise, with goals for

Left: It is important in all forms of training and training exercises to take advice from a qualified instructor before embarking on a rigorous training regime. As all players have their own individual characteristics, strengths and weaknesses, it is important that any training and fitness schedules should be tailored to meet your personal requirements. As a general rule, train — don't strain. Start with light loads and a sensible number of repetitions. These can be built up gradually as your level of fitness improves. It is important to warm up thoroughly with gentle stretching prior to beginning work on strength exercises like these in order to reduce the possibility of injuries and muscle strain. The exercises shown here are designed mainly to strengthen ligaments and muscles. They are press-ups and squat thrusts (top), swallows (above left) and sit-ups (left).

improvement, is more beneficial than that done at random, but all exercise is of value. So think *fitness*, and think *exercise*, so that using the body actively becomes a lifelong habit. Remember that a fit body helps the mind to be alert.

Warm up exercises

In all forms of suppleness exercises begin by stretching gradually until the stretch feels slightly uncomfortable. Hold this position for 10 seconds and then relax and repeat. You should work methodically through the different body areas and muscle groups. In general, you should start from the head and work down to the feet, or vice versa.

Neck stretches *(right) Stand with feet apart and push your head slowly down to one side, stretching out your neck. Hold for 10 seconds. Move your head up slowly to the centre, and then repeat to the other side. Do 5 repetitions each side.*

Shoulder and tricep stretches *(right) Raise your right arm above your right shoulder and lower it to touch your shoulder blade behind you. Use your other arm to push your right elbow backwards until you feel some tension. Hold for 10 seconds. Relax and repeat with the left arm. Do 5 repetitions each side.*

1

2

Hamstring stretch
(far left)
Stand upright, legs straight and feet together. Interlock your hands behind your thighs and slowly slide them down past your knees as low as you can extend them on your calves until you feel the tension in the muscles. Hold for 10 seconds. Relax and repeat 5 times.

Shoulders warm up *(left)*
Stand with one arm outstretched straight in front of you. Raise it slowly to the sky, rotate backwards in a circular motion down to your side and then raise it to regain the original position. Repeat 5 times. Relax and repeat 5 times with the other arm.

The lunge *(left)*
Take up the lunge position shown here with the back leg extended with the knee straight and the heel firmly on the ground to stretch the calf muscles. Keeping your body upright, bend your front leg almost at 90 degrees. Feel the stretch in your trailing leg and hold for 10 seconds. Relax and repeat 5 times with each leg. To stretch your Achilles tendon, slightly bend the knee of the trailing leg but keep your toes flat on the ground.

Back and hips warm up
(right)
Stand with your feet apart and arms raised straight above your head. Then turn the upper body only from the waist to one side and slowly stretch downwards, lowering your outstretched arms as far as possible until it starts to feel uncomfortable. Hold for 10 seconds and slowly regain your upright position. Relax and repeat to the other side. Do 5 repetitions each side.

1

2

3

4

Hamstring stretch *(left)*
Stand with your feet crossed and, with your fingers interlaced, stretch out your arms to their full extent in front of you. Slowly bend from the waist, trying to reach down as far as possible. Hold for 10 seconds. Slowly regain your upright position, cross your feet the other way. Repeat 5 times each side.

Ankles warm up *(left)*
Stand on one foot and raise your other foot off the ground. Slowly move the raised foot in a clockwise circular motion. Do 10 rotations and then repeat with 10 rotations in an anti-clockwise direction. Relax and repeat with the other foot.

1

2

Groin and hamstring stretch *(right)*
Stand with feet wide apart. Bend from the waist to touch the ground in the centre. Bend to the left, come up slowly and bend to the right. Then, with arms outstretched to each side, touch both ankles together. Get your head as low as possible. Relax and repeat 5 times. 1

Hamstring stretch *(left)*
Sit on the ground with your legs wide apart. Bend over slowly from the waist stretching out your arms until your hands reach your ankles, lowering your head towards your knee until you feel slight discomfort. Hold for 10 seconds. Slowly regain an upright position and repeat to the other side. Then slowly regain the upright position and stretch into the middle. Repeat 5 times.

1

2

3

Chapter 10 **Techniques**

Stroke technique: the way to tactical success

When you watch top class players in action you will see that they use a very wide variety of different techniques and styles of play. This makes it extremely difficult for the interested observer to work out which style or choice of technique will be the most effective. More importantly it creates a problem for him in deciding which approach it would be best for him to copy to improve his own game.

Because there is no single, definitive technique for hitting a particular shot, not even a definitive way of holding the racket, making a decision on this basis can be confusing. There is a variety of methods of play, all of which are being used successfully by world class players. For example, on the backhand side, Ivan Lendl always plays one-handed, Jimmy Connors always plays two-handed, and Mats Wilander plays with two hands when attacking but often plays with one hand when defending!

The whole area of technique can develop into a minefield of confusion in the mind of the average player. There is the service to consider, as well as groundstrokes, volleys, smashes, lobs, drop shots and the like, all of which call for specific techniques. Add

to these the variations of spin, the different methods of holding the racket and other technical considerations which are mentioned in this book, and you will have an idea of the sheer amount of knowledge and understanding which a player requires to perform at the highest level.

The principles of technique
However, underpinning all the top players' techniques are certain fundamental principles that need to be considered. Every player needs to establish for himself a method of performance that is sound and dependable, and which can be used repetitively and dependably.

A sound technique will enable you to hit the ball well and to aim successfully towards your target areas. This provides you with a firm platform for your chosen strategy and tactical objectives.

You can decide for yourself on the method of play that you wish to develop, either by copying a player whom you respect, or by experimenting with different methods until you feel comfortable with a particular technique. Of course, if you are copying a

Groundstrokes

Left: Hitting positions/ contact point for the forehand drive (Eastern grip). In pictures 1 and 2 the player is hitting the ball at a comfortable distance from the body and slightly forward of the leading hip. In picture 1 the ball is being played at waist height; in picture 2 it is played at knee height.

Left: Hitting positions/ contact point for back-hand drive (backhand grip). In both pictures the player is hitting the ball at a comfortable distance from the body and slightly forward of the leading foot. The ball is played at waist height in picture 1; and played at knee height in picture 2.

particular player, you should make sure that his or her physical and mental characteristics are not too different from your own.

Remember the fundamentals

Whatever method you choose and whoever you attempt to copy, you will find that there are certain fundamental principles of technique that apply to all shots, whether you are just beginning to play tennis or whether you are a more experienced player. These fundamentals are interlinked.

● Watch the ball carefully, judging its speed, height and bounce. This will help you to move into a sound position in good time to play your shot.

● Develop good footwork in order to reach the ball and set up an effective hitting position.

● Remember that good balance will be necessary, especially when you are actually hitting the ball, to ensure that your shot is controlled.

● Smooth racket movement, on any particular shot is important. Develop this through repetition until you have the necessary control, feel, and power.

● Aim the racket head, when you contact the ball, directly towards the target area.

If you can manage to achieve a good ratio of success in applying these fundamentals to your own personal technique you will find that you are not just *looking* a better player, but you will be giving yourself the opportunity actually to *become* a better player. Do not forget, however, that technical skills in isolation do not win the points. The secret is to use these skills in matchplay to support your strategy and tactics.

The forehand drive

There are three types of forehand drive: lifted, topspin and sliced. The most orthodox way of hitting this stroke uses the Eastern grip. Adjustments to the path of the swing using a Continental, Semi-Western or Western grip are suggested later (see pages 132 and 133).

For all types of strokes a comfortable hitting position is the first priority. Practise moving accurately in relation to the flight path of the ball.

The lifted drive
While moving from an alert readiness position to gain a comfortable hitting position for the lifted drive, start a sideways turn towards the ball. As you approach your hitting position, take the racket back in good time to be able to swing your racket head 'through' the ball. Prepare for your hitting position on the right foot, and step in with the left foot as you swing from your shoulder, so transferring weight into the shot. Turning from the hips as you swing will add power as well as aiding balance. Turning the hips and shoulder will bring your chest round, facing the net, as you complete the shot and follow through.

The racket head should rise during the stroke, so take it to a position below the intended point of impact before you start the forward swing, and follow through with a sense of lift. The racket should cross in front of your body during the follow through, then catch it at its throat with the other hand, ready to move into position for the next shot. Throughout a practice, check that you are moving into a comfortable hitting position for each stroke as it is only from these that the stroke can gain maximum effect at all levels of play.

With all types of drive, aim to clear the net by two or three feet when you are aiming for length. Lower the trajectory of the ball when you want to hit to a shorter length, or when your

opponent is at the net, as the lower ball will be difficult for him to volley.

The topspin drive
To add topspin to a lifted drive, swing with greater lift, while brushing the racket strings sharply up the back of

1

4

the ball. The forward rotation of the ball (topspin) can be aided by slightly closing the racket face after impact (for a definition of 'open' and 'closed' see page 132). The strings should brush up and behind the ball.

The sliced drive

For slice, the racket head must start above the point of impact, with its face slightly open. Direct the swing downwards, so causing the strings to brush slightly under the ball, giving it backward rotation. The amount of slice is controlled by the degree to which the racket face is opened and the downward path of the swing. The more steeply downwards the racket is swung, the greater the spin on the ball.

The lifted forehand drive *(left)*
1 *Early racket preparation is essential.*
2 *The beginning of the forward swing.*
3 *The racket head is below the ball with the weight going into the shot.*
4 *Contact point at a comfortable distance from the body.*
5 *The weight going into the shot.*
6 *The balanced follow through.*

The grip

An *open* racket face is one which is tilted back with the hitting side pointing upward. A *closed* face is one which is tilted forward to show the hitting side to the ground.

The Eastern grip

The Eastern grip makes the racket a natural extension of the arm, so the face of the racket is parallel to the palm of the hand. If the racket is held in an Eastern grip its face can be closed by turning the wrist to the left and opened by turning the wrist to the right, but there is no natural inclination for it to be either open or closed.

The various other grips alter the racket face in relation to the palm of the hand, so adjustments to the wrist, and to swing path must be made in order to control the ball as desired.

Alternative grips

The Continental grip, which is similar to the service grip illustrated on page 138, slightly opens the face of the racket, while the Semi-Western and Western cause the racket face to close.

When playing a lifted drive with a Continental grip the racket face has to be adjusted by turning the wrist a little to the left to neutralize the face of the racket. Otherwise, the combination of a rising swing and an open faced racket will lift the ball more than is intended. For topspin, the wrist must be turned rather more to the right to close the face of the racket while the path of the swing must also be adjusted. Start the swing below the point of impact, as with the Eastern grip, but the follow through should feel like following the rim of a hoop, up and over the ball and then down. The Continental grip is an ideal grip for slice.

With the closed racket face caused by the Semi-Western grip, a normal rising swing might not lift the ball sufficiently for it to clear the net. So there must be a strong feeling of lift during the swing. Many players find this lift easier to achieve when played from a more open stance, with the follow through coming more sharply across the body. The closed face makes the Semi-Western grip ideal for topspin, particularly off higher bounc-

The Semi-Western forehand drive

The Semi-Western forehand drive *(right)*
1 *Alert position of readiness.*
2 *Early preparation of the racket.*
3 *Full extension of the racket backswing.*
4 *Preparing to swing from well beneath the ball.*
5 *Contact point.*
6 *The follow-through imparting topspin.*

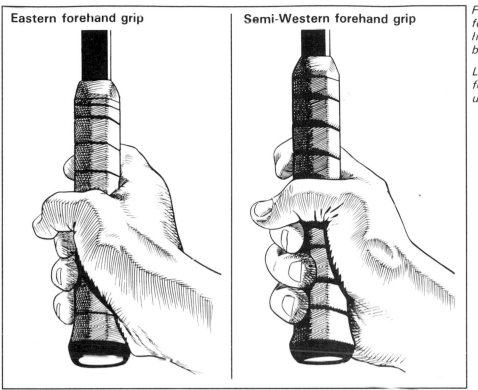

Eastern forehand grip

Semi-Western forehand grip

Far left: The Eastern forehand, or 'shake-hands', grip with palm beneath the handle.

Left: The Semi-Western forehand grip with palm underneath the handle.

ing balls which do not need so much lift to clear the net. It is not suitable for sliced strokes because a large wrist adjustment has to be made to open the face of the racket, the slice feels awkward to play, and power is lost.

The characteristics of the Western grip are the same as for the Semi-Western, but more exaggerated. It is good for topspin against higher bouncing balls, not very effective against lower bouncing ones, as so much lift is needed, and not suitable for sliced shots.

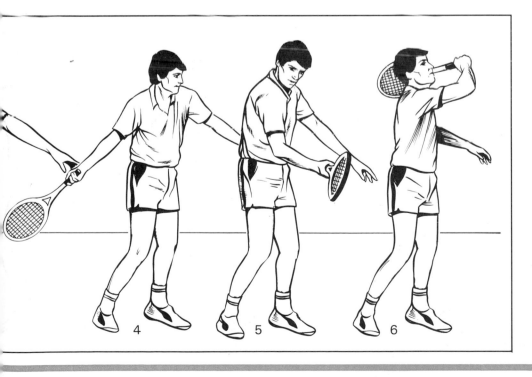

133

The backhand drive

1

The lifted backhand drive *(right and opposite)*
1 Early preparation.
2 Full backswing prior to lowering the racket head for lift.
3 Just before contact, eyes on the ball, a comfortable distance away.
4 The weight going into the shot.
5 The balanced follow through.

The backhand drive is struck as though you were hitting the ball with the back of your hand. It needs a grip which feels strong behind the handle of the racket so, as in the diagram, the grip is turned to the left, from the forehand grip, until the thumb is slanting across the back of the racket handle, and the wrist is over the top of it.

Only with such a grip, or with two hands, can the wrist be braced during the shot. If the wrist is weak the racket head may drop and be out of control, so a supporting grip is essential

Lifted backhand drive

The path for this stroke is similar to the forehand, but of course played on the other side of the body. Take your racket hand back near to your left leg, with your hitting arm close to your body. The racket head must be below the intended point of impact, so you can use a rising swing, following through across the body and finishing with the racket pointing high to your right.

To add topspin to a lifted drive, lift the racket more steeply during the rising swing to brush up the back of the ball. In addition the racket face can be slightly closed after impact.

Sliced backhand drive

For a sliced drive, start the forward swing from a higher take-back position so that you can hit slightly down and under the ball. You must turn your wrist so that the racket face opens as you strike the ball.

For all types of backhand drives it is essential to turn sideways so that you have a free space to swing through at the side of your body. The grip must be firm, but not tight, and the wrist allowed free movement. It should neither be locked, nor too loose, or racket head control suffers. Swing the racket head right through the ball.

Choose wisely

The choice of lift, topspin or slice depends on the type of ball you are about to play, and what you want from the shot. If you can attack, lift or top-spin are preferable, while if you have to defend, slice is easier to play when under pressure.

Most players have a preference for one of the types of backhand drive. Use the stroke you feel most confident with, but practise all three and add them to your technical armoury.

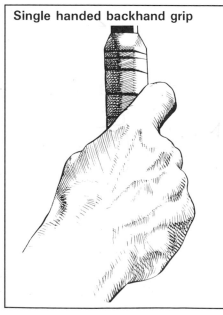

Single handed backhand grip

Right: The Single handed backhand grip with the palm on top of the handle, fingers spread and thumb diagonally across the back.

Two-handed play

The main advantage of two-handed play is that racket control is improved by the extra strength and support from the second hand. Those who have sufficient strength to control the racket with one hand on the backhand as well as the forehand can choose whether to use one or two hands as preferred. For very young players, it is preferable to start with two hands on the backhand, although this is rarely really necessary for the forehand. If the grip and wrist are not strong enough to control the racket on a one-handed backhand, frustration occurs and a fear of playing backhand shots can become instilled. But those who start with two-handed backhands may change to playing with one hand later on when their strength and confidence have developed.

The two-handed backhand

Keep the two hands close together on the racket handle, with the right hand below the left for the right handed player. Position yourself a little nearer to the ball than for one handed play, since using two hands restricts the reach slightly.

A shorter take-back can be used, because of the greater available strength and this is a useful aid in disguising the direction of the shot. The top hand grip should be the same as a forehand one and the two hands should work in harmony.

The grip for the lower hand may be changed from a forehand grip to a backhand one (see diagram). The advantages of this change are greater racket control, and having a backhand grip ready for those shots which you may be forced to play with one hand because the ball is too wide to be reached with two hands on the racket.

A recent trend is for some two-handed players to use both hands for lifted and topspin drives, and one hand for slice. Mats Wilander's change to this method stimulated many to follow his very successful example.

The different styles

Watch top players who use two hands to learn more about their various methods, but never copy one slavishly. Develop a style of your own, with which you feel comfortable.

Most two-handed players do not

The two-handed backhand *(right)*
1 *The readiness position.*
2 *Early preparation.*
3 *Stepping into the shot.*
4 *Forward swing with the racket head coming up to meet the ball.*
5 *Contact point.*
6 *The balanced follow through.*

The two handed backhand

1   2   3

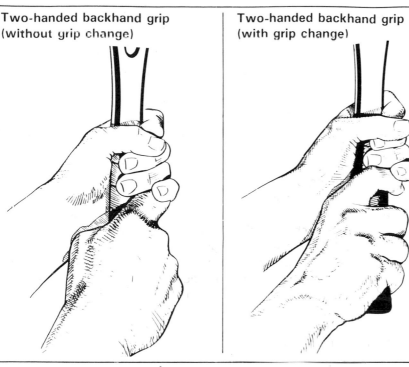

Two-handed backhand grip (without grip change)

Two-handed backhand grip (with grip change)

Far left: The two-handed backhand (without grip change) shows two Eastern forehand grips, with the palm behind the handle.

Left: In the two-handed backhand (with grip change) the right hand uses the backhand grip whereas the left hand uses the Eastern forehand.

turn sideways as much as one handed ones, so the shot is played with the follow through more across the body rather than directly towards the net. Those whose style is to follow through further in the direction of the shot, take off the top hand just after impact.

The take-back of the racket is almost invariably lower with two hands than it is with one. This is ideal for lifted or topspin shots but awkward for slices, where the racket has to be lifted above the intended point of impact before the forward swing. The change in take-back is a signal to the opponent that slice is about to be played.

The drive volley is a popular and effective stroke from two handed players, because of the extra strength and control.

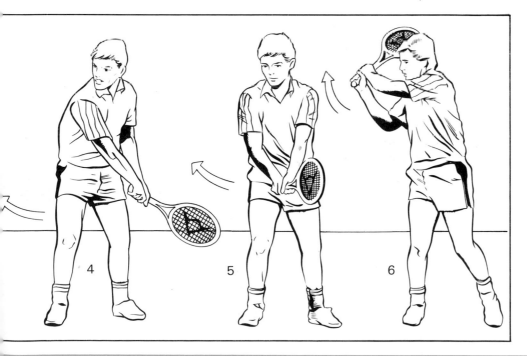

The basic service

Your normal service should be played with a chopper grip and its technique kept as simple as possible. Do not imitate the style of some top players who have developed parts of their service action which suit *them*, but are unlikely to suit many who copy them. John McEnroe's highly individual stance, Boris Becker's leap into court, and some accentuated backhand grips which have been developed to gain extra spin are unlikely to be beneficial to most players, but imitating them while developing a service can be a definite handicap to a player's progress.

It can be rewarding to experiment once you have gained a sound basic service, with a straightforward action, a well-placed ball, and good balance throughout the stroke. But do not try too many variations before you have a consistent delivery which you can rely on in your matches.

Develop sound principles

The throwing action used in serving is similar to the one you use for the throwing of a ball forward and high

1

into the air, with an overhand action. The ball should be placed a little to the hitting side of the server and as high as he can reach with the top edge of the racket frame.

The two hands should work in smoothly together, with the aim of striking the ball with the centre of the racket strings while the throwing arm is at full stretch. Impact should be made after the ball has dropped a very short distance.

The place-up

For the place-up, rest the ball lightly in the fingers of your left hand, and push the arm up slightly ahead and to the right of your body. At the same time take the racket back to start the overhead throwing action. Release the ball just before your left arm comes to full upward stretch. Practise synchronizing the two actions. When practising, do not complete the throwing action of the racket unless the place-up of the ball is accurate. Let the ball drop, and try again.

Stance and balance

As your place-up, racket head throwing action, and timing of these two skills improve, develop your stance and pay more attention to balance.

Your stance, if you are right-handed, should be with your left foot in front of the right, about a shoulder's-width

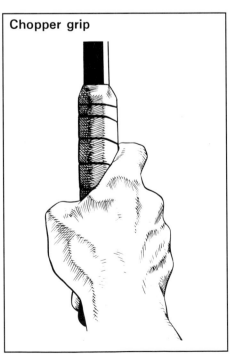

Chopper grip

Right: The Chopper grip is approximately half-way between the Eastern forehand and the backhand grips.

The basic service *(left)*
1 *Rhythmical and smooth placement of the ball.*
2 *The ball at full height prior to the throwing action of the racket.*
3 *Contact point — the player reaching as high as possible.*
4 *The weight following the direction of the ball.*
5 *Moving towards net.*

apart. When serving to the deuce court place the back foot a very little to the right of the front one, slightly to the left when serving into the advantage court. Place the ball in light contact with the racket strings, turning your shoulders so you are facing the net.

Make yourself comfortable, and take careful aim at your target in the service court. Bring your weight very slightly forward as you prepare to serve, and transfer it to the back foot as you take the racket back. Bring the weight forward again in harmony with the throwing action.

Quickly regain your balance, ready for your next stroke. If you are serve-and-volleying, use the impetus of your serve to bring you in towards the net.

Before every service you should check your balance, put the ball and racket strings together, take aim, and then serve. This ritual gives you the best chance of settling your balance and your mind, instead of rushing in, ill prepared, to start the new point.

Service variations

The slice serve
(right and opposite)
1 *A comfortable starting position.*
2 *Placement of the ball slightly to the right and forward.*
3 *The ball at full height prior to the throwing action of the racket.*
4 *Just before impact with the racket face at an angle to impart slice.*
5 *The balanced follow through.*

Have a good understanding of the basic service before attempting to develop variations. To develop two, or three, types of service at the same time can be confusing.

Progress is quicker if you develop a basic service to a good standard, and then adjust your technique to use slice or topspin as an alternative delivery. Choose one of the variations to develop, and start on the other only when you have made good progress with your first choice. If you are left handed, simply reverse the instructions that follow.

1

The slice service
Adjust the place-up so that the ball is a little further to the hitting side, and the same height as for the basic service.

The second adjustment to be made for slice is to the angle of the racket face. The racket should be kept on edge while throwing its head to slice round the side of the ball. The ball will be rotated by contact with the strings, causing it to swerve to the left, and continue this swerve after bouncing.

The third adjustment is to the path of the racket. From the bent-arm position the racket should be thrown a little out to the right so that its strings can brush round the outside of the ball. The follow through should be more circular than for the basic service, coming across the body and finishing well to the left of it.

When aiming with a slice service, allowance must be made for the swerve of the ball.

To vary the amount of slice vary the angle of the racket: more angled for more slice, flatter for less. Practise hard to master the slice service; using it occasionally is a good way to deceive your opponents.

The topspin service
Place the ball up a little to the left of your body, and further back than for the basic service. If a practice place-up is allowed to fall, the ball should drop very near to the baseline and a little to the left of your feet.

Bend from the trunk to the left, also bending your knees as you take your racket back. You should still be able to see the ball which has been placed up to your left.

Throw the racket head, on its edge as in the slice, upwards and well to your right, brushing up and across the back of the ball. The upward brushing of the ball creates topspin and the sideways brushing puts sidespin on it. The topspin causes the ball to dip sharply towards the end of its flight, giving a higher bounce than for a basic service. The sidespin causes the ball to break away to the right. The ball will be struck when it is rather lower than for the other services, so a feeling of lift is needed in the throwing action.

The upward strike sends the ball high over the net, with the topspin control bringing it down into the court. The awkward bounce may cause problems for your opponent, and it is good service to follow to the net, being slower through the air and giving you more time to gain a good volleying position.

The break after landing is useful for attacking the left side of the opponent's court when serving to the advantage court.

2

3

4

5

Volleys

The balls that you volley are travelling faster than those which have bounced, so preparation for volleys must be performed quickly with a very short take-back of the racket from the readiness position. Instead, the racket is taken upwards and then forwards for the volley.

High forehand volley

Pick the racket up from the readiness position so that it is pointing almost directly upwards with your arm bent at the elbow: diagonally if the ball is further away. Meet the ball while it is still between you and the net, straightening your arm to punch down on it. Watch the ball right on to your racket, avoiding the temptation to look away at your intended target. The downward angle of the punch will depend on the height of the ball and its distance from the net at impact. The grip should be Eastern or Continental, with the racket held firmly but not too tightly. Stepping in with the left foot as you play the volley will add to its power through weight transference.

High backhand volley

This, too, should be played at a comfortable distance from you, and the ball should be met out in front instead of being allowed to come alongside you. The shot is played with a backhand grip for control.

Intead of the racket head pointing directly upwards it should be taken back and a little lower than on the forehand side by bending the arm sharply at the elbow. By straightening the arm with a snap, power is given to the stroke. As with the forehand, aim is obtained by punching the racket head in the direction of the shot. Adjust-

The high volley *(right and far right) These pictures show the firm racket and arm movement necessary to control the ball. Notice how at the end of the shot the player has managed to keep his balance and is ready to recover to a strong net position.*

The low volley
(left and below left)
The pictures show the poise and balance required to get down to the low volley. Notice how the ball is played well in front of the body, thus facilitating the player's movement to the net.

ment of the body position and the wrist turn can aid directional control.

Low volleys

A low volley is one which cannot be struck downwards because of the height of the ball, or your distance from the net: it directs the ball straight, or upwards to clear the net. Start the stroke with the racket head above or behind the ball instead of below it, as with lifted drives. The ball is controlled by opening the face of the racket before impact. The turned-back face will lift the ball, while the block or short punch stroke directs it forwards.

Practise volleying

As you improve with each type of volley, intersperse your practices with volleying against another volleyer. This will speed reaction and recovery, as well as getting you used to a series of random and assorted volleys.

Lobs

For the basic lob, on either forehand or backhand, adapt your normal lifted drives to guide the ball to a high trajectory. Start with the racket lower in relation to the intended point of impact so that the ball can be lifted more than when playing a normal ground stroke, and follow through high to bring the racket head pointing almost directly upwards. Make the stroke long and smooth, *feeling* the ball on the strings as you lift it.

Height

Vary the height of lobs depending on the tactic you are using, but always lob to drop the ball near to the opponent's baseline. If your purpose is to drive your opponent back from the net, aim to clear his upward reach while allowing for a backward movement and jump. So a high, very deep lob is generally your objective.

Lob much higher if you need time to reposition yourself after having been driven well outside your sidelines by a wide ball. Lob very high, too, when your opponent has the sun in his eyes, as then he will have longer to look at the ball.

The attacking lob

If your intention is to clear the net player with a lower lob which is *just* out of his reach, use topspin. If you have got the ball over him and he is chasing back, the topspin will cause the ball to move away from him quickly after it has bounced, and it could be an outright winner.

Apply topspin to a strongly lifted shot by rotating the strings up the back of the ball, keeping your wrist flexible. You can also apply topspin by sharply lifting the racket head to brush up the back of the ball, finishing the follow through high above your head. You have to make a very fast racket swing to give the ball sufficient forward impetus if you wish to hit a deep shot using topspin.

The defensive lob

Against attacking shots such as the smash or very aggressive volleys, the defensive lob is often the best reply. It is also a very useful shot as a variation, particularly in doubles, as a return of service when the server has followed in to the net. Turn back the face of the

The lob *(right)*
1 *Preparing the racket early.*
2 *Stepping into the ball.*
3 *The racket head below the height of the ball.*
4 *Contact point with a slightly open racket face to give height.*
5 *The balanced follow through.*

The lob

1   2   3

Left: A good picture of a player who has been lobbed successfully and is trying to race back to play the ball after it has bounced.

racket and play similarly to a low volley, but with a much longer follow through in an upwards direction. The open racket face, as well as the path of the racket head, will direct the ball upwards to clear the net player.

Aim to drop the ball near to the opponent's baseline from a height greater than for basic or attacking lobs. The opponent will almost always go for a smash against a defensive lob, so make the smash as difficult as you can for him. Apart from concentrating on length you should direct the ball to his backhand side when that is possible. By making your defensive lob a high one, your opponent will find it difficult to time his shot, as the ball will be dropping quickly when it reaches him.

The lob is an excellent tactical shot if it is played well, but can be a gift to your opponent if it is short of length. So practise playing lobs boldly, rather than tentatively. It is quite difficult for your opponent to judge whether a deep lob will be in or out, and he is tempted to volley it if he can reach it. A short lob is always easier to play.

4   5

The smash

The smash action is similar to the service action, but with a shorter take-back of the racket. When serving you are hitting a ball which is hardly moving and which you have placed for yourself, while when smashing the ball has been placed by your opponent. Another challenge is that, as the ball will be dropping from a height, it will be moving quickly so your timing will be tested.

However, you have two advantages when smashing rather than serving. One is that you have an area much larger than the service court into which to aim, and the other is that you play your smashes nearer to the net, so it is less of an obstacle.

The action
● Turn sideways and move quickly to intercept the falling ball. Bring your racket up into a throwing position, behind your back.

● Adjust your position by rapid foot movements to get into a comfortable hitting position in relation to the ball: it should be dropping just to your hitting side.

● Throw the racket head up to meet the ball at full stretch, striking it while it is a little nearer to the net than you are. Try to get the feel of hitting over it, and smashing it down, by snapping your wrist forwards just before you make contact with the ball.

● Follow through across the body, bringing your racket head down to almost sweep the ground.

Recover your readiness position, and regain your position in the court, ready for a possible return.

The smash (below)
1 *Early take-back of the racket.*
2 *Full extension prior to the throwing action of the racket.*
3. *Contact point at full stretch.*
4 *The balanced follow through with the weight going into the shot.*

The smash

1   2   3   4

Smash tactically

Against a short lob a very powerful smash away from your opponent, or a sharply angled controlled smash, is undoubtedly the best answer. If the lob is very short you may be able to play a smash which bounces the ball right out of court, making it unreturnable. Use a lot of power, and a very flexible wrist to bring the strings well over the top of the ball, and aim to place the ball near to your opponent's service line so that it gets a very high bounce from the sharply downward path of its trajectory.

Spin variations

Using the same principles as for the slice service, the slice smash from the deuce court runs the ball out to the side of your opponent's deuce court. Another variation is to use modified topspin, or you can position yourself directly underneath the falling ball, bend slightly to your left and strike the ball on its left hand side. The follow through will come down to the right hand side of your body.

Modify aggression

If the lob against you is very deep, you will be unlikely to hit a winner from well back in your court. Use less wrist snap and play firmly for placement rather than full power keeping the pressure on your opponent, who may give you a better chance for a powerful smash later. Against very high lobs or if the sun is blinding you, it is wiser to let the ball bounce, and then smash it if the bounce is high enough. This is, of course, a more defensive tactic as you will be further from the net than if you had smashed before the bounce, and your opponent is given more time to prepare for his reply.

Below: A good action photo of a player playing a forehand smash slightly left of centre. It is advisable to play the stronger forehand smash where possible rather than the backhand smash.

Drop shot, stop volley and soft volley

The three shots outlined below exploit the space near to the net when the opponent is near his baseline. If you can disguise the coming drop shot or stop volley, your opponent will delay his start forward, reducing his chance of reaching the ball.

There is no need to disguise the soft volley. Play this when your opponent is stranded, with no hope of reaching a short length ball. It is a safer shot to play than the stop volley, so use it when a firm but soft shot to the other side of the court into the open space is a certain winner.

The drop shot

This shot is played with a delicate touch to produce a low pace shot which drops just over the net, clearing it by its own height. The comparatively high clearance over the net ensures that the ball drops down, instead of towards the incoming opponent. Backspin will further check the forward bounce, and the wind in your face is another great help. Prepare by positioning yourself and taking your racket back as though you were going to drive. Check the pace of your swing while opening the racket face by turning back your wrist. The contact with the ball should be from below, so causing it to rise off the strings, and creating backspin.

In practice, learn the amount of pace

Right: Ivan Lendl, very close to the net having just played a stop volley, shows the poise and balance necessary for this delicate shot.

Opposite: Arantxa Sanchez takes a chance from a position just inside the baseline and plays a very difficult drop shot. She demonstrates perfect balance, concentration and subtle control.

you need to play balls of differing speed. A very open racket face will take more pace off the ball than one which is only just open. Against a fast ball you can rely entirely on controlling the rebound off the strings, but with a slow ball you will have to swing to clear the net.

The stop volley

This shot, too, needs a sensitive touch to take nearly all the pace off your opponent's drive. Play it from close to the net, first preparing as for a normal volley and disguising your intentions. Check the punch and open the racket face just before contact, hitting almost directly underneath the ball. The ball should leave the strings upwards, but with just enough forward pace to clear the net. The strings brushing underneath the ball create backspin, which will check its forward bounce.

For both these shots use your normal grip. Wrist control is also important as many mistakes are made by players trying to put on excessive backspin by loosening the wrist more than is necessary.

The soft volley

Play this shot in the same way as normal volleys but with gentle control. The rebound off the strings plus a firm but gentle push is sufficient to control the ball with the aid of a volley through in the direction of your target area.

These shots are often called *touch shots* because of the need for a sensitive touch between the racket strings and the ball as they are played. Practice should be concentrated on taking the pace off the ball by cushioning it on the strings at impact, while applying a little backspin to check the bounce. Tactically there is no need to take the risk of trying to drop the ball very close to the net if your opponent is really far back in his court. Play the percentages according to how far you, and your opponent, are from the net. Although these shots are gentle ones they should be played with the same *mental* aggression as power shots.

Recovery shot: lob, drive and half volley

The recovery shot

This is played in response to a good lob or lob volley against you. With no chance of playing a smash, your only hope is to turn and chase after the ball. Run a little to one side so that your shot is not hampered. If you can catch the ball in time to turn towards it before you strike, then a good percentage shot is a drive. But if you can only *just* reach the ball while still facing the back of the court, then a lob can be hooked back over your shoulder. Aim for where you sense is the middle of your opponent's court, as aiming blindly you need the biggest margin for error possible. Lob high to give you time to recover.

Lob volley

The lob volley is of particular use in doubles, when all four players are volleying from well inside the service courts. The situation for its use in singles occurs less frequently, but it is useful as an occasional surprise shot.

The intention of the lob volley is to direct the ball well over the head of an opposing volleyer. Prepare as though about to play a normal volley, but as the racket head is near to impact, turn back the strings and follow through upwards to lift the ball. Practise to aim lob volleys to land reasonably near to the opponent's baseline, and high enough to just clear his outstretched racket. If they are too high the opponent will be able to get back under them and smash, while you are still in a vulnerable position near to the net.

Drive volley

This variation from the basic volley is often very successful for the two handed player. The technique is simply to play a lifted or topspin drive before the ball has bounced. Shorten the racket take-back but follow through normally. If you are near the net and the ball arrives about shoulder height, the shot can be played very aggressively. Further from the net, and with the ball lower, the shot should now be semi-aggressive as the ball has to be kept in court.

The drive volley is a good tactical shot against a steady baseline player, played from around the service line as an angled attacking shot. It is also useful as an approach shot, since it is

Below: Mats Wilander is about to play a half volley at full stretch. Notice how in this instance his grip is more on top of the racket than usual (almost a backhand grip). This allows him to rescue the ball from a late hitting position.

played nearer to your opponent than a groundstroke approach. With less time to play his return, your opponent should be further pressurized by your determined move towards the net.

Half volley

This is a shot in which the ball is hit immediately after it has bounced. Use normal groundstrike technique, with a shorter take-back than for a drive, and ensure that the knees are well bent to get down for the shot. Play firmly but not too aggressively, as the sharp incline from the low point of impact needs to be carefully controlled to keep the ball in court. An alternative method is to play the half volley with an open racket face and very restricted follow through. For a soft return, or a drop shot, the upward rebound off the strings should be aimed to just clear the net.

You should never play the half volley by choice, but it is an invaluable shot to play against a ball which you intended to volley low, but which lands shorter than expected. It is also useful against a strong deep drive from your opponent. If you are at the back

Above: Kevin Curren shows a beautiful example of a forehand drive volley. Notice how he has jumped off the ground in order to get the necessary height above the ball and attack it with maximum force.

Left: Boris Becker is about to play a half volley from just behind the service line. Notice the vertical angle of the racket face which will enable him to contact the ball squarely and firmly and keep it low over the net.

of the court and have not enough time to move back to play a normal drive off a higher ball, or want to retain an attacking position on court, hold your ground and play a half volley from a balanced position.

Improving technique

There are a number of suggestions for drills, games and competitions, and match practices in Chapter 9. For them all, comfortable hitting and early racket preparation are essential for success. If you watch any inexperienced group of players trying to rally in pairs, it becomes obvious that the main causes of error are playing from off-balance or cramped hitting positions, and by strokes being rushed because they are taken too late.

Preparation and timing

Prepare your position well and have your racket ready to play your stroke without rushing, and the stroke will have the best possible chance of success. Of course these two vital aspects of preparation are not sufficient by themselves to guarantee success. The stroke has to be started at the right time to meet the ball in the most comfortable place. Clean impact on the ball has to be made, and a smooth follow through for control and direction, is the final essential.

Stroke fundamentals

These fundamentals apply to all strokes. Use them as a checklist when you are practising to improve technique. Select your weak fundamentals and work to improve them, as each affects the others.

- *Watch the ball*. Keep your eyes on it as you strike, to get a clean hit.
- Good *footwork* takes you to a comfortable position in relation to the ball.
- Good *balance* aids movement, and provides stability for aiming.
- Control of the *way* in which you are using racket, swing, throw, slice, etc.
- Control of the racket, by the *grip* and use of the *wrist*, during the stroke.

If all five are performed well together, from a comfortable hitting position and with good timing, your stroke will be an efficient one. Provided you aim well, while using a

Below: This picture shows a method of practice to improve technique with four players on the court. The court is divided down the middle into two narrow singles courts thereby allowing two separate practices to take place at the same time. The baseline players are practising their drives, whereas the volleyers are practising their technique while aiming at the targets.

fundamentally sound stroke, then the resulting shot will be effective.

Recover quickly to be in time to prepare for the next shot. Enjoy your practices for stroke development. You will gain more improvement from them if you concentrate on one aspect of your technique at a time. If you try to improve several aspects at once, confusion will arise as your mind will be roving from one part of the overall skill to another, and back again. Progress will be much slower than if you master, for example, comfortable hitting, and then control of the swing, or another relevant aspect, prior to transferring the improvement into the whole skill.

Develop your own styles of stroke play, but never neglect the importance of the five fundamentals, which are a common factor to *all* successful styles.

Above: Ivan Lendl shows the results of years of disciplined practice and training. His movement and his positioning have been stretched on a wide ball and yet he still manages to maintain balance and control of his sound technique.

Equipment

Tennis players do not need much equipment. The basic requirements are suitable courts to play on, someone to play with, suitable clothing, a racket, a ball and, if you are playing out of doors as most people still do, reasonably good playing conditions!

Shoes

Your shoes are the most important part of your tennis equipment, more important even than the racket. Tennis playing is a supremely athletic activity, not just involving running at speed in straight lines, but with constant changes in direction, checking from speed, skidding sometimes on the court surface, jumping at angles dictated by the position of the ball, not by the player. Consequently it is very demanding on the feet and lower limbs.

The modern tennis shoe performs four main functions.

● Protection for the feet against injury and strain.
● Cushioning, through the sole, from jarring on the court surface.
● Grip for mobility and stopping power.
● Support for the ankles.

Your shoes should have enough room for your toes, should fit comfortably at the heel, waist and girth, should 'breathe' well and should have adequate padding and inner soles to provide good shock protection.

There should be no question of economizing on tennis shoes, and you should buy the best pair you can afford, preferably from a specialist supplier who can advise you on your choice. Most medium range tennis shoes these days are supplied with a fairly uniform sole pattern, or 'tread', commonly a herringbone pattern, and are suitable for any surface.

Right: The pattern on the sole of a general purpose tennis shoe is suitable for most outdoor surfaces (left) and can be compared with the smoother sole (right) more suitable for indoor play. Some indoor facilities require you to have shoes that protect the court and give the best grip on specialized indoor surfaces.

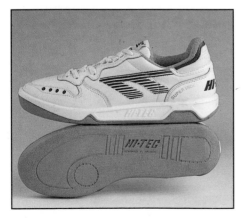

These days a number of top players have adopted the cross trainer as an alternative to a shoe designed specifically for tennis. These are shoes which are suitable for other sports as well as tennis, and are designed to provide a maximum of support and stability. They are acceptable for tennis as long as their soles will not harm the court surface – a very important consideration. Finally, if you are going to play mainly indoors, you should check that the type of shoes you have for outdoor play are suitable for use on the indoor surface. Some facilities have special requirements to protect the surfaces from the damage that can be caused by grit and dirt, and you may have to have a separate pair for indoor use, maybe of a special sole type.

Rackets

The racket is more than just an implement for hitting the ball. It should become an extension of your body, almost a part of you. It follows that it must be of the right weight for your build, and it must have good balance.

Instead of being weighed in ounces, rackets are now supplied 'light', 'medium' and 'heavy'. You should not buy a racket that is too heavy for your build, as a heavy racket will not, in itself, give you a powerful serve or increase the pace of your strokes. Indeed if your racket is too heavy you will simply tire quickly, and the difficulty you will have in controlling the racket will have the effect of undermining your control and accuracy when playing your shots. However if you are strongly built, the extra weight of a heavy racket will add power to your shots.

As with shoes, buy the best quality you can afford and be guided not only by the retailer, but by a coach or tennis professional if possible.

Balls

Any decent quality ball you buy will conform to official specifications, although you should on no account buy cheap or unbranded balls, that

have been mass produced to low standards.

It is worth considering why tennis balls are changed so frequently at Wimbledon and other major tournaments. When struck hard, the ball deforms alarmingly, becoming almost flat, and after this process has been repeated a large number of times, even the best balls suffer a noticeable impairment in bounce.

Clothing

What you wear for tennis is very much a matter of personal choice and style these days, as there is no longer any requirement to wear white only, for example.

Men's shorts have pockets, and these are useful for keeping the second service ball out of the way, but it is important to check that they are cut so that you won't catch your hand or the butt of your racket on them in play. Shirts and tops likewise should be loose enough to give free movement but not so loose that they could impede the racket.

Above: Modern tennis clothing is light and attractive. Remember that appearance is not as important as having comfortable and absorbent material against the skin. Your clothes should not restrict you in any way. Today's rackets are made from highly durable and consistent materials; make sure you choose a racket that is just the right weight for you and feels well balanced.

Tournaments

Many players are content to play purely for enjoyment, with friends or relations, and have no desire to compete seriously. For most people, however, and especially the young, progress in their tennis playing standard leads them on to seek at least some taste of the thrills of the great tournaments, which they may have experienced through the medium of television. For them, there are many types of tennis tournament, with scope for of all ages and abilities.

Club ladders

Players are placed on a ladder in the club in order of merit, the best being number one and the highest number being allocated to the least experienced. They are allowed to challenge approximately three places above and, if they win, they go into the position above the player they have just beaten and everybody else on the ladder goes down a place. This is a very good system for the players to find their level within the club.

Club leagues

These are similar in concept to the ladder. All the players start off in leagues in approximate order of merit. Generally, five or six players form a league with each player playing against each other member of the league. At the end of a set period of time, perhaps three or four weeks, the league is complete, with players in order of merit. The winner is promoted to the league above and the bottom player is relegated to the league below. The league then recommences for the next set period of weeks.

Knock-out tournaments

These are tournaments where, if there are 32 players in a draw, the 32 players are paired off into 16 matches for round one. After round one, the 16 winners go into round two. They are paired off into eight matches to produce eight winners for round three, and so on until there is a final winner. The first round losers will play one match, the second round losers will play two matches etc., and this is why it is called a knock-out tournament.

American tournaments

In American tournaments everybody plays everybody else and the winner is the one with the greatest number of points. The score will be two for a win and one for a draw. In an American tournament of eight people, everybody will play seven matches and there will be a total of 28 matches played altogether. At the end of the American tournament it is possible to make a ranking list of players based upon the final results table.

Round Robin tournaments

These are similar to American tournaments and are often used when the numbers in an American tournament are too few, or if the entry is so large that it must be split into smaller sections of say four or five, and each section plays a Round Robin. For example, with 24 players there are four separate groups of six. Each group will play an American tournament amongst its group members which will result in four winners emerging. The winners will then either go into another group Round Robin to find the winner or into a knock-out competition.

Postal tournaments

Postal tournaments are tournaments where there is no central venue for each match. Players are drawn to play matches on either a 'home' or 'away' basis. The home players arrange the venue, balls etc. and the away player has to travel to the home player's choice of venue. The result of the match is posted to the organizer who informs the winners of the draw for the next round of matches.

Ratings tournaments

The intention of a ratings tournament is to provide a contest in which players of a similar standard are drawn together in groups to compete against each other in the initial stages. The winners of a section receive prizes and qualify for the next stages of the tournament amongst the higher rated players. The tournament generally lasts two weeks at one venue and each rating section is completed in approximately three to four days. At the end of the first section, the winners of that section qualify to go through to compete in the higher rating section over the next three to four days. When this rating section is completed, the winners again go through. The top rated players do not enter the competition until the last three days, while the other players have been playing through to meet them.

A player's rating will govern which section of the draw he is placed in. The player's initial rating will be ascertained by the information supplied. Players may be re-rated during the season at any time if they have been placed in a section that is not suitable to their standard.

Closed tournaments

These are tournaments that are 'closed' to a certain category of membership. For example, a club closed tournament will only accept competitors from its membership and not from outsiders. The closed tournament can take varied forms, such as knock-out or Round Robin.

Open tournaments

This is a tournament open to all players. It has no restrictions and it is possible that a novice may play a national player in the first round. The competition can again take various forms.

Satellite tournaments

These are a series of tournaments run by the Governing Body for players who are trying to become full-time professional tennis players and who wish to break into the Grand Prix tennis circuit.

There are generally pre-qualifying tournaments for the satellite competitions. The winners of the satellite earn computer points which may qualify them for direct entry into Grand Prix tournaments and ATP (Association of Tennis Professionals) and WITA (Womens International Tennis Association) and ITF (International Tennis Federation) tournaments.

Club team competitions

The team members normally represent a club in singles or doubles, in league competitions or in knock-out competitions. The competitions played may include county league up to national knock-out competitions and national league competitions.

Index

Index continued

Acknowledgements

The publishers would like to thank the players who demonstrated strokes and exercises for the special photographs, taken by Tommy Hindley at the U.K. National Training Centre, Bisham Abbey:

Andy Mills   Anna Greenwood
Rachel Neal   Marc Curtis
Gary Stewart   Andy Poole
Andrew Baker

Our thanks also to Wilson Sporting Goods Co. and Hi-Tec Sports UK Ltd. for the use of the photographs in the Equipment section.